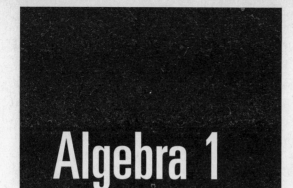

Algebra 1

LARSON
BOSWELL
KANOLD
STIFF

Applications • Equations • Graphs

Notetaking Guide

The Notetaking Guide contains a lesson-by-lesson framework that allows students to take notes on and review the main concepts of each lesson in the textbook. Each Notetaking Guide lesson features worked-out examples and Checkpoint exercises. Each example has a number of write-on lines for students to complete, either in class as the example is discussed or at home as part of a review of the lesson. Each chapter concludes with a review of the main vocabulary of the chapter. Upon completion, each chapter of the Notetaking Guide can be used by students to help review for the test on that particular chapter.

McDougal Littell
A HOUGHTON MIFFLIN COMPANY
Evanston, Illinois • Boston • Dallas

ISBN-13: 978-0-618-41021-7   ISBN-10: 0-618-41021-X

12 13 14 15–DOM–08

Contents

Algebra 1 Notetaking Guide

Contents

Contents

Contents

1.1 Variables in Algebra

Goals • Evaluate a variable expression.
• Write a variable expression that models a real-life situation.

VOCABULARY

Variable

Values

Variable expression

Evaluating the expression

Unit analysis

Verbal model

> To evaluate an expression, use the following model.
>
> Write the variable expression.
> ↓
> Substitute values for variables.
> ↓
> Simplify the numerical expression.

Example 1 — *Evaluating a Variable Expression*

Evaluate the expression when $x = 3$.

a. $6x$ **b.** $\dfrac{9}{x}$ **c.** $x + 4$ **d.** $13 - x$

Solution

a. $6x = 6(\underline{\quad})$ Substitute ___ for x.
   $= \underline{\quad}$ Simplify.

b. $\dfrac{9}{x} = \dfrac{9}{\boxed{}}$ Substitute ___ for x.

   $= \underline{\quad}$ Simplify.

c. $x + 4 = \underline{\quad} + 4$ Substitute ___ for x.
   $= \underline{\quad}$ Simplify.

d. $13 - x = 13 - \underline{\quad}$ Substitute ___ for x.
   $= \underline{\quad}$ Simplify.

Example 2 — *Evaluating a Real-Life Expression*

Average speed is given by the following formula.

$$\text{Average speed} = \frac{\text{Distance}}{\text{Time}} = \frac{d}{t}$$

Find the average speed (in miles per hour) of a car that traveled 240 miles in 6 hours.

$\text{Average speed} = \dfrac{d}{t}$ Write expression.

$= \dfrac{}{}$ Substitute ____ for d and ___ for t.

$= \underline{\quad}$ Simplify.

Answer The average speed was ___ miles per hour.

✓ *Checkpoint* **Complete the following exercises.**

1. Find the average speed of a car that traveled 200 miles in 4 hours.	**2.** Find the average speed of a truck that traveled 120 miles in 2 hours.

Example 3   *Evaluating a Geometric Expression*

Geometry Connection Find the perimeter of the triangle. The dimensions are in inches.

$b = 12$
$a = 5$
$c = 13$

> The perimeter of a triangle is equal to the sum of the lengths of its sides: $a + b + c$.

Solution

Perimeter $= a + b + c$ Write expression.

$= \underline{\quad} + \underline{\quad} + \underline{\quad}$ Substitute values.

$= \underline{\quad}$ Simplify.

Answer The triangle has a perimeter of _____.

Example 4   *Finding Time*

Jogging You plan to jog at an average rate of 4 miles per hour for a distance of 3.2 miles. How long will it take you?

Solution

Verbal Model   Time $= \dfrac{\boxed{}}{\boxed{}}$

Labels   Time $= t$ (hours)

                    Distance $= \underline{\quad}$ (miles)

                    Rate $= \underline{\quad}$ (miles per hour)

Algebraic Model $t = \underline{}$ Write algebraic model.

                    $= \underline{\quad}$ Simplify.

Answer It should take you about ____ hour(s).

✔ *Checkpoint* **Find the perimeter of the triangle with the indicated side lengths. The dimensions are in feet.**

3. $a = 12$, $b = 16$, $c = 20$	**4.** $a = 20$, $b = 21$, $c = 29$

5. You plan to ride your bicycle at an average rate of 8 miles per hour for a distance of 12.8 miles. How long will it take you?

1.2 Exponents and Powers

Goals • Evaluate expressions containing exponents.
• Use exponents in real-life problems.

VOCABULARY

Power

Base

Exponent

Grouping symbols

Example 1 *Reading and Writing Powers*

Express the meaning of the power in words and then with numbers

Solution

Exponential Form	Words	Meaning
a. 15^1		
b. 5^2		
c. 6^3		

Example 2 *Evaluating Powers*

Evaluate the expression x^5 when $x = 2$.

Solution

$x^5 = \underline{}^5$ Substitute ___ for x.

$ = \underline{}$ Write factors.

$ = \underline{}$ Multiply.

Example 3 *Evaluating an Exponential Expression*

Evaluate the expression $(a - b)^4$ when $a = 5$ and $b = 3$.

Solution

$(a - b)^4 = (\underline{} - \underline{})^4$ Substitute ___ for a and ___ for b.

$ = \underline{}^4$ Subtract within parentheses.

$ = \underline{}$ Write factors.

$ = \underline{}$ Multiply.

Example 4 *Evaluating an Exponential Expression*

Evaluate the expression $(a^2) + (b^2)$ when $a = 7$ and $b = 4$.

Solution

$(a^2) + (b^2) = (\underline{}^2) + (\underline{}^2)$ Substitute ___ for a and ___ for b.

$ = \underline{} + \underline{}$ Evaluate powers.

$ = \underline{}$ Add.

✔ *Checkpoint* **Evaluate the expression for the given value of the variable.**

1. $3^n + n^3$ when $n = 5$	2. $(3c^4 - 18)^c$ when $c = 2$

Order of Operations

> **Goals** • Use the order of operations to evaluate algebraic expressions.
> • Use a calculator to evaluate real-life expressions.

VOCABULARY

Order of operations

| **Example 1** | *Evaluating Without Grouping Symbols* |

Evaluate the expression $4x^2 + 3$ when $x = 3$.

Solution

$$4x^2 + 3 = 4 \cdot \underline{}^2 + 3 \qquad \text{Substitute } \underline{} \text{ for } x.$$

$$= 4 \cdot \underline{} + 3 \qquad \text{Evaluate power.}$$

$$= \underline{} + 3 \qquad \text{Evaluate product.}$$

$$= \underline{} \qquad \text{Evaluate sum.}$$

| **Example 2** | *Using the Left-to-Right Rule* |

Operations that have the same priority, such as multiplication and division *or* addition and subtraction, are performed using the *left-to-right rule*, as shown in Example 2.

a. $28 - 7 - 4 = (28 - 7) - 4 \qquad$ Work from left to right.

$$= \underline{} - 4$$

$$= \underline{}$$

b. $15 + 9 \div 3 - 4 = 15 + (9 \div 3) - 4 \qquad$ Divide first.

$$= 15 + \underline{} - 4$$

$$= (15 + \underline{}) - 4 \qquad \text{Work from left to rig}$$

$$= \underline{} - 4$$

$$= \underline{}$$

ORDER OF OPERATIONS

1. First do operations that occur within _____ .

2. Then evaluate _____ .

3. Then do multiplications and _____ from left to right.

4. Then do _____ and subtractions from left to right.

Example 3   *Using a Fraction Bar*

$$\frac{5 \cdot 3}{13 + 6^2 - 4} = \frac{5 \cdot 3}{13 + \boxed{} - 4}$$ Evaluate power.

$$= \frac{\boxed{}}{13 + \boxed{} - 4}$$ Simplify the numerator.

$$= \frac{\boxed{}}{\boxed{} - 4}$$ Work from left to right.

$$= \frac{}{}$$ Subtract.

$$= \frac{}{}$$ Simplify.

✔ *Checkpoint* Evaluate the expression for the given value of the variable.

1. $29 - 4b$ when $b = 6$	**2.** $18 - \dfrac{42}{c}$ when $c = 7$

Evaluate the expression.

3. $2 \cdot 3^2 + \dfrac{4}{7}$	**4.** $[22 - (4^3 \div 8)] \cdot 3$

Example 4 *Using a Calculator*

When you enter the following in your calculator, does the calculat
display 8.7 or 4.3?

6.4 + 12.8 ÷ 3.2 − 1.7 ENTER

Solution

a. If your calculator uses order of operations, it will display 8.7.

$$6.4 + 12.8 \div 3.2 - 1.7 = 6.4 + (12.8 \div 3.2) - 1.7$$
$$= 6.4 + \underline{} - 1.7$$
$$= \underline{} - 1.7$$
$$= \underline{}$$

b. If your calculator displays 4.3, it performs the operations as the
are entered.

$$[(6.4 + 12.8) \div 3.2] - 1.7 = (\underline{} \div 3.2) - 1.7$$
$$= \underline{} - 1.7$$
$$= \underline{}$$

✓ *Checkpoint* **Two calculators were used to evaluate an
expression. The calculators gave different results. Which
calculator used the established order of operations? Rewrite
the expression with grouping symbols so that both calculator
give the correct result.**

5. 6 + 12 ÷ 4 − 4 ENTER	Calculator A: 0.5
	Calculator B: 5
6. 14 − 6 ÷ 2 × 3 ENTER	Calculator A: 5
	Calculator B: 12
7. 4 × 6 − 24 ÷ 3 ENTER	Calculator A: 0
	Calculator B: 16

1.4 Equations and Inequalities

Goals • Check solutions and solve equations using mental math.
• Check solutions of inequalities.

VOCABULARY

Equation

Solution of an equation

Inequality

Solution of an inequality

Example 1   *Substituting to Check Possible Solutions*

Check whether the numbers 1, 2, and 3 are solutions of the
equation $2x + 3 = 5$.

Solution

Substitute each possible solution into the equation. If both sides of
the equation are the same value, then the number is a solution.

x	$2x + 3 = 5$	Result		Conclusion	
1	$2(\underline{}) + 3 \overset{?}{=} 5$	_____	1	_____	a solution.
2	$2(\underline{}) + 3 \overset{?}{=} 5$	_____	2	_____	a solution.
3	$2(\underline{}) + 3 \overset{?}{=} 5$	_____	3	_____	a solution.

Example 2 *Using Mental Math to Solve a Real-Life Equation*

School Supplies A box of pencils costs $3.08, a package of per
costs $3.45, and a notebook costs $2.79. You have $8. About hov
much more money do you need?

Solution

You can ask the question: The total cost equals _____
_____? Let x represent any additional money you
may need. Use rounding to estimate the total cost.

$$3 + 3.5 + 3 = 8 + x$$

$$\underline{} = 8 + x$$

Answer Because the total cost of the supplies is approximately
_____ or $_____ , you can see that you need about $_____ more.

Example 3 *Checking Solutions of Inequalities*

Decide whether 3 is a solution of the inequality.

a. $x + 5 < 9$ **b.** $3x + 2 \le 11$ **c.** $x - 1 > 4$

Solution

Inequality	Substitution	Result	Conclusion
a. $x + 5 < 9$	$\underline{} + 5 \overset{?}{<} 9$	_____	3 _____ a solution.
b. $3x + 2 \le 11$	$3(\underline{}) + 2 \overset{?}{\le} 11$	_____	3 _____ a solution.
c. $x - 1 > 4$	$\underline{} - 1 \overset{?}{>} 4$	_____	3 _____ a solution.

✓ *Checkpoint* Check whether the given number is a solution of
the equation or inequality.

1. $4d + 1 = 9$; 2	**2.** $5n - 7 < 23$; 6	**3.** $x^2 + 6 \ge 55$; 7

1.5 A Problem Solving Plan Using Models

Goals • Translate verbal phrases into algebraic expressions.
• Use a verbal model to write an algebraic equation or inequality to solve a real-life problem.

VOCABULARY

Modeling _____

Mathematical model

OPERATION	VERBAL PHRASE	EXPRESSION
Addition	The _____ of six and a number	_____
	Eight _____ a number	_____
	A number _____ five	_____
	A number _____ by seven	_____
Subtraction	The _____ of five and a number	_____
	Four _____ a number	_____
	Seven _____ a number	_____
	A number _____ by nine	_____
Multiplication	The _____ of nine and a number	_____
	Ten _____ a number	_____
	A number _____ by three	_____
Division	The _____ of a number and four	_____
	Seven _____ by a number	_____

> Order is important for subtraction and division. "Four less than a number" is written as $x - 4$, not $4 - x$.

Example 1   *Writing an Algebraic Model*

You and your friends go to a video store to buy DVDs on sale for $12.50 each. Together, you buy 6 DVDs and you spend $79.50, which includes tax. Use mental math to solve the equation for how much tax you paid.

Solution

Verbal
Model

$$\boxed{} = \boxed{} \cdot \boxed{} + \boxed{}$$

Labels   Total cost = _____   (dollars)

Cost per DVD = _____   (dollars)

Number of DVDs = ___   (DVDs)

Tax = t (dollars)

Algebraic   _____ = _____ · ___ + t
Model
          _____ = _____ + t

          _____ = t

Answer You and your friends paid $_____ in tax.

A PROBLEM SOLVING PLAN USING MODELS

Verbal
Model

Ask yourself what you need to know to solve the problem. Then write a _____ that will give you what you need to know.

Labels

Assign labels to each part of your verbal model.

Algebraic
Model

Use the labels to write an algebraic model based on your verbal model.

Solve

Solve the algebraic model and answer the _____ question.

Check

Check that your answer is _____ .

Example 2 **Using a Verbal Model**

You are running in a marathon at a speed of 5 miles per hour. After 3 hours, you have run 15 miles. If you maintain your current speed, how long will it take you to run the last 11.2 miles of the marathon?

Solution

a. Use the formula $Time = \dfrac{Distance}{Rate}$ to write a verbal model.

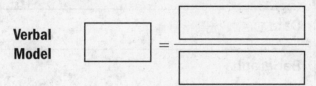

| **Verbal
Model** | ☐ = | ⬚⬚⬚⬚⬚⬚ |

Labels   Time = t (hours)

Distance = _____   (miles)

Your speed = _____   (miles per hour)

**Algebraic
Model** $t = \dfrac{\;\square\;}{\;\square\;} = $ _____

Answer If you maintain your current speed, it will take you _____ hours to finish the marathon.

✔ *Checkpoint* **Complete the following exercises.**

1. In Example 2, is it reasonable to expect that you can finish the entire marathon in 5 hours running 5 miles per hour?

_____

2. **Fundraising** The science club is selling magazine subscriptions at $12 each. How many subscriptions does the club have to sell to raise $276? Use the problem solving plan to answer the question.

1.6 Tables and Graphs

Goals
- Use tables to organize data.
- Use graphs to organize data.

VOCABULARY

Data

Bar graph

Line graph

Example 1 *Using a Table*

The data in the table were taken from a study on how much people in the United States spend for cable and satellite television. In which 1-year period did the amount spent for cable and satellite television increase the most?

Solution

Enter the amount of change from one year to the next.

Amount spent by Americans for cable and satellite television (dollars per person per year)					
Year	1996	1997	1998	1999	2000
Amount	$136.96	$153.11	$165.56	$179.89	$192.82
Change	_____	_____	_____	_____	_____

Answer From the table, you can see that the greatest increase occurred from _____ to _____ . During that period, the amount spent per person for cable and satellite television increased by $_____ .

Example 2 *Interpreting a Bar Graph*

The bar graph shows the amount Americans spent for cable and satellite television in a given year.

Explain why the graph could be misleading.

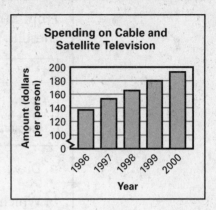

Solution

The bar graph could be misleading because _____

_____

_____

_____

_____

_____

✔ *Checkpoint* **Complete the following exercises.**

1. In which 1-year period from Example 1 did the amount spent for cable and satellite television increase the least?

_____

2. Draw a new bar graph for Example 2 that would not be misleading.

Example 3 *Making a Line Graph*

From 1993 to 1999, the average school spending per student in the U.S. is given in the table.

Average School Spending Per Student							
Year	1993	1994	1995	1996	1997	1998	1999
Amount	$5804	$5996	$6208	$6443	$6764	$7142	$7533

a. Draw a line graph of the data.

b. Which year showed the greatest increase?

Solution

a. Draw the vertical scale from 0 to _____ dollars. Use units of ___ for the vertical axis to represent intervals of _____ dollars. Draw the horizontal axis and mark the number of years starting with _____. For each amount in the table, draw a _____ on the graph. Draw a _____ from each _____ to the next _____.

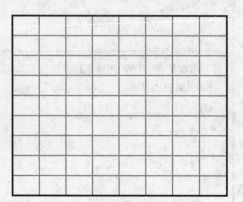

b. The greatest increase in the average school spending per student occurred in _____.

1.7 An Introduction to Functions

Goals • Identify and make an input-output table for a function.
• Write an equation for a real-life function.

VOCABULARY

Function

Input

Output

Domain

Range

Example 1 *Making an Input-Output Table*

a. Make an input-output table for $y = x^2$ using $x = 0, 1, 2,$ and 3.

b. Does the table represent a function? Justify your answer.

c. Describe the domain and the range.

Solution

a. Evaluate $y = x^2$ for $x = 0, 1, 2,$ and 3.

Input x	0	1	2	3
Output y				

b. _____ , because for each _____ there ___ exactly one _____ .

c. The domain is the collection of all input values _____ .
   The range is the collection of all output values _____ .

1. Make an input-output table for $y = 2x - 1$ using $x = 1, 2, 3,$ and 4. Does the table represent a function? Justify your answer. Describe the domain and range.

Example 2 *Graphing a Function*

Use the function $y = 17 + 10x$, where $0 \leq x \leq 4$.

a. For several inputs x, use the function to calculate an output y.

b. Make a line graph of the function.

Solution

	INPUT	FUNCTION	OUTPUT
a.	$x = 0$	$y = 17 + 10(\_\_)$	$y = \_\_\_\_$
	$x = 1$	$y = 17 + 10(\_\_)$	$y = \_\_\_\_$
	$x = 2$	$y = 17 + 10(\_\_)$	$y = \_\_\_\_$
	$x = 3$	$y = 17 + 10(\_\_)$	$y = \_\_\_\_$
	$x = 4$	$y = 17 + 10(\_\_)$	$y = \_\_\_\_$

b. The _____ are the graph of the table data. The _____ is the graph of the function.

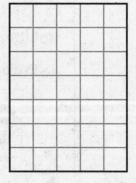

Example 3 *Writing an Equation*

Auto Repair To fix a car, a mechanic estimates that it will take 2 to 5 hours of work and $270 in parts. The mechanic charges $35 per hour. Represent the total cost of the repair C as a function of the hours h that it takes the mechanic to fix the car for every hour starting with 2 hours and ending at 5 hours. Write an equation for the function. Then make an input-output table for the function.

Solution

> Apply the problem solving strategy from Lesson 1.5.
> * Write a verbal model
> * Assign labels
> * Write an algebraic model

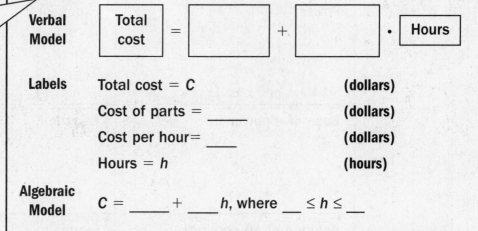

Verbal Model

| Total cost | = | | + | | · | Hours |

Labels

Total cost = C (dollars)

Cost of parts = ____   (dollars)

Cost per hour = ___   (dollars)

Hours = h (hours)

Algebraic Model

$C =$ ____ $+$ ____ h, where ___ $\leq h \leq$ ___

Use the equation to make an input-output table for the function.

Hours h	2	3	4	5
Total cost C				

✔ *Checkpoint* **Complete the following exercise.**

2. a. You are buying fabric that costs $6.40 per yard. Write an equation for the total cost of the fabric C as a function of the yards of fabric y that you buy.

   b. Make an input-output table for the function for every 5 yards until you reach 30 yards.

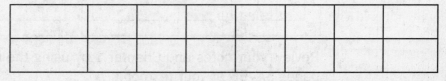

Words to Review

Give an example of the vocabulary word.

Variable expression	Verbal model
Power	Exponent
Base of a power	Equation
Solution of an equation	Inequality
Function	Input-output table
Domain	Range

Review your notes and Chapter 1 by using the Chapter Review on pages 54–56 of your textbook.

The Real Number Line

Goals • Graph and compare real numbers using a number line.
• Find the opposite and the absolute value of a number.

VOCABULARY

Real numbers

Real number line

Negative numbers

Positive numbers

Integers

Graph

Plotting

Opposites

Absolute value

Velocity

Counterexample

Example 1 *Comparing Real Numbers*

Graph -3 and -7 on a number line. Then write two inequalities that compare the two numbers.

Solution

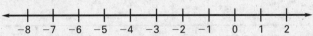

On the graph, -7 is to the _____ of -3, so -7 is _____ -3.
On the graph, -3 is to the _____ of -7, so -3 is _____ -7.

Answer -7 ___ -3 and -3 ___ -7.

Example 2 *Ordering Real Numbers*

Write the following numbers in increasing order: $-\dfrac{4}{5}$, 1.8, $\dfrac{3}{2}$, -1.

Solution Graph the numbers on a number line.

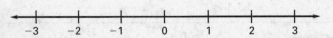

Answer From the graph, you can see that the order is

_____ .

Example 3 *Finding the Opposite of a Number*

Find the opposite of -4.

Solution

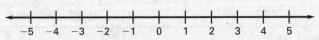

Answer The opposite of -4 is ___ because -4 and ___ are on opposite sides of the origin and are both ___ units from the origin.

THE ABSOLUTE VALUE OF A NUMBER

- If a is a positive number, then $|a| = $ ___ .
  Example: $|10| = $ ___

- If a is zero, then $|a| = $ ___ .
  Example: $|0| = $ ___

- If a is a negative number, then $|a| = $ ___ .
  Example: $|-10| = $ ___

Example 4 *Solving an Absolute Value Equation*

Use mental math to solve the equation.

a. $|x| = 3$ **b.** $|x| = -2$

Solution

a. The numbers _____ are __ units from the origin, so there are _____ solutions: _____.

b. Because distance is _____ negative, the absolute value of a number is _____ negative, so there is _____.

Example 5 *Using a Counterexample*

Decide whether the statement is *true* or *false*. If it is false, give a counterexample.

a. The expression $|a|$ is *sometimes* greater than a.

b. The expression $-|a|$ is *always* less than a.

Solution

a. _____

b. _____

_____

✔ **Checkpoint** Complete the following exercise.

1. Compare $-|-4|$ and 4 using <, >, or =.

2.2 Addition of Real Numbers

Goals • Add real numbers using a number line or addition rules.
• Use addition of real numbers to solve real-life problems.

Example 1 *Adding Three Real Numbers*

Use a number line to find the sum: $-2 + (-7) + 10$.

Solution

$-2 + (-7) =$ ____

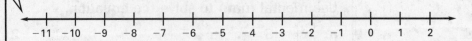

Start at ____.

To add -7, move __ units to the ____.

To add 10, move ____ units to the _____.

End at __.

Answer The sum can be written as $-2 + (-7) + 10 =$ __ .

RULES OF ADDITION

To Add Two Numbers with the *Same Sign*:

1. Add their _____.

2. Attach the _____ sign.

Example: $-4 + (-5)$ **Step 1** $|-4| + |-5| = 9$ **Step 2** ____

To Add Two Numbers with *Opposite Signs*:

1. _____ the _____ absolute value from the _____ absolute value.

2. Attach the sign of the number with the _____ absolute value.

Example: $3 + (-9)$ **Step 1** $|-9| - |3| = 6$ **Step 2** ____

PROPERTIES OF ADDITION

Commutative Property The order in which two numbers are added does not change the sum.

$a + b =$ ___ $+$ ___   Example: $3 + (-2) =$ ____ $+$ ___

Associative Property The way you group three numbers when adding does not change the sum.

$(a + b) + c =$ ___ $+ ($ ___ $+$ ___ $)$

Example: $(-5 + 6) + 2 =$ ____ $+ ($ ___ $+$ ___ $)$

Identity Property The sum of a number and 0 is the number.

$a + 0 =$ ___   Example: $-4 + 0 =$ ____

Property of Zero The sum of a number and its opposite is 0.

$a + (-a) =$ ___   Example: $5 +$ _____ $= 0$

Example 2   *Finding a Sum*

> Using the properties of addition can help make computation more efficient. For example, by adding 2.3 and 4.7, you get a whole number.

a. $2.3 + (4.7 + 1.2) = ($ ____ $+$ ____ $) +$ ____   Use associative property.

$=$ ___ $+$ ___   Simplify.

$=$ ___

b. $-\dfrac{2}{3} + 6 + \dfrac{2}{3} = 6 +$ _____ $+$ ___   Use commutative property.

$= 6 + \left[+ \right]$ Use associative property.

$= 6 +$ ___   Use property of zero.

$=$ ___   Use identity property.

✔ *Checkpoint* **Use the rules of addition to find the sum.**

1. $1.2 + (-8) + 2.8$	**2.** $\dfrac{3}{4} + 3 + \left(-\dfrac{3}{4}\right)$

Subtraction of Real Numbers

Goals • Subtract real numbers using the subtraction rule.
• Use subtraction of real numbers to solve real-life problems.

VOCABULARY

Terms

SUBTRACTION RULE

To subtract b from a, add the opposite of b to a.

$a - b = \underline{} + (\underline{})$ **Example:** $3 - 5 = \underline{} + (\underline{})$

The result is the _____ of a and b.

Example 1   *Evaluating Expressions*

Evaluate the expression $-5 - 3 - (-1) - 5$.

Solution

$-5 - 3 - (-1) - 5$

$= -5 + \underline{} + \underline{} + \underline{}$ Add the opposites of 3, -1, and 5.

> Use the left-to-right-rule.

$= \underline{} + \underline{} + \underline{}$ Add -5 and ____.

$= \underline{} + \underline{}$ Add ____ and ___.

$= \underline{}$ Add ____ and ____.

Example 2   *Finding the Terms of an Expression*

Find the terms of $-3 - 8x - y$.

Solution Use the subtraction rule.

$-3 - 8x - y = -3 + (\underline{\hspace{1cm}}) + (\underline{\hspace{1cm}})$ **Rewrite the difference as a sum.**

Answer The terms of the expression are _____, _____, and _____.

✔ *Checkpoint* **Complete the following exercises.**

1. Evaluate $1 - 2 - (-3)$.	2. Find the terms of $-8 - 7x$.

Example 3   *Evaluating a Function*

Evaluate the function $y = 2x - 3$ for these values of x: $-2, -1, 0$, and 1. Organize your results in a table and describe the pattern.

Solution

Input	Function	Output
$x = -2$	$y = 2(\underline{\hspace{0.7cm}}) - 3$	
$x = -1$	$y = 2(\underline{\hspace{0.7cm}}) - 3$	
$x = 0$	$y = 2(\underline{\hspace{0.7cm}}) - 3$	
$x = 1$	$y = 2(\underline{\hspace{0.7cm}}) - 3$	

Answer Each time x increases by 1, y _____.

Example 4 *Using a Calculator*

Use a calculator to evaluate the expression $-2.91 - (-3.18)$.

Solution

Keystrokes	Display
2.91 [+/-] − 3.18 [+/-]	_____

Answer $-2.91 - (-3.18) =$ _____

✔ *Checkpoint* **Complete the following exercises.**

3. Evaluate the function $y = -x$ for these values of x: -2, -1, 0, 1, and 2. Organize your results in a table and describe the pattern.

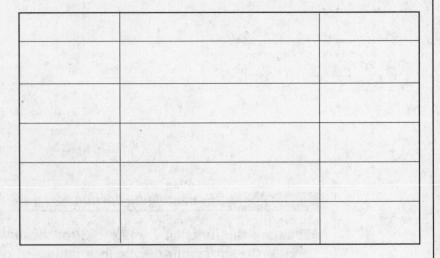

4. Use a calculator to evaluate the expression
$-3.84 - (-1.57) + 4.86$.

2.4 Adding and Subtracting Matrices

Goals • Organize data in a matrix.
• Add and subtract two matrices.

VOCABULARY

Matrix

_____

Entry or element

Example 1   *Writing a Matrix*

Basketball Write a matrix to organize the basketball statistics for the first half of a game.

Player A   8 points, 1 rebound, 2 assists, 1 steal
Player B   3 points, 0 rebounds, 2 assists, 2 steals
Player C   6 points, 1 rebound, 1 assist, 1 steal

Solution

Player A, *Player B*, and *Player C* can be labels for the rows or for the columns.

P = points
R = rebounds
A = assists
S = steals

A = Player A
B = Player B
C = Player C

As row labels:

$$\begin{array}{c c c c c}
 & P & R & A & S \\
A & & & & \\
B & [\underline{\quad}\ \underline{\quad}\ \underline{\quad}\ \underline{\quad}] \\
C & & & &
\end{array}$$

As column labels:

$$\begin{array}{c c c c}
 & A & B & C \\
P & & & \\
R & & & \\
A & [\underline{\quad}\ \underline{\quad}\ \underline{\quad}] \\
S & & &
\end{array}$$

Example 2 | *Adding and Subtracting Matrices*

Use the matrix you wrote in Example 1. The matrix for the second half of the game is given below.

a. Find the sum of the first half matrix and the second half matrix.

b. Find the difference of the first half matrix and the second half matrix.

Solution

a.

First Half
$$
\begin{bmatrix} \underline{\ } & \underline{\ } & \underline{\ } & \underline{\ } \\ \underline{\ } & \underline{\ } & \underline{\ } & \underline{\ } \\ \underline{\ } & \underline{\ } & \underline{\ } & \underline{\ } \end{bmatrix}
$$
$+$
Second Half
$$
\begin{bmatrix} 9 & 4 & 3 & 0 \\ 2 & 1 & 0 & 1 \\ 7 & 2 & 0 & 3 \end{bmatrix} =
$$

Entire Game
$$
\begin{bmatrix} \underline{\ }+9 & \underline{\ }+4 & \underline{\ }+3 & \underline{\ }+0 \\ \underline{\ }+2 & \underline{\ }+1 & \underline{\ }+0 & \underline{\ }+1 \\ \underline{\ }+7 & \underline{\ }+2 & \underline{\ }+0 & \underline{\ }+3 \end{bmatrix} = \begin{matrix} A \\ B \\ C \end{matrix}
$$

	P	R	A	S
A	__	__	__	__
B	__	__	__	__
C	__	__	__	__

b.

First Half
$$
\begin{bmatrix} \underline{\ } & \underline{\ } & \underline{\ } & \underline{\ } \\ \underline{\ } & \underline{\ } & \underline{\ } & \underline{\ } \\ \underline{\ } & \underline{\ } & \underline{\ } & \underline{\ } \end{bmatrix}
$$
$-$
Second Half
$$
\begin{bmatrix} 9 & 4 & 3 & 0 \\ 2 & 1 & 0 & 1 \\ 7 & 2 & 0 & 3 \end{bmatrix} =
$$

> The difference matrix shows the differences between each players' statistics between the first and second halves.

Difference
$$
\begin{bmatrix} \underline{\ }-9 & \underline{\ }-4 & \underline{\ }-3 & \underline{\ }-0 \\ \underline{\ }-2 & \underline{\ }-1 & \underline{\ }-0 & \underline{\ }-1 \\ \underline{\ }-7 & \underline{\ }-2 & \underline{\ }-0 & \underline{\ }-3 \end{bmatrix} = \begin{matrix} A \\ B \\ C \end{matrix}
$$

	P	R	A	S
A	__	__	__	__
B	__	__	__	__
C	__	__	__	__

✔ *Checkpoint* **Find the sum or difference of the matrices.**

1. $[2 \quad -3] - [-1 \quad 7]$

2. $\begin{bmatrix} 5 & -7 \\ -1 & 3 \end{bmatrix} + \begin{bmatrix} 6 & 2 \\ 8 & -12 \end{bmatrix}$

2.5 Multiplication of Real Numbers

Goals • Multiply real numbers using properties of multiplication.
• Multiply real numbers to solve real-life problems.

THE SIGN OF A PRODUCT

• A product is negative if it has an _____ number of negative factors.
• A product is positive if it has an _____ number of negative factors.

Example 1   *Multiplying Real Numbers*

a. $2 \cdot 3 = $ ___   Zero negative factors; _____ product

b. $7(-7)(-2) = $ ___   Two negative factors; _____ product

c. $(-2)^3(-1)^2 = $ ____   Five negative factors; _____ product

d. $-3^2(-5) = $ ___   Two negative factors; _____ product

> In Example (d), be sure you understand that 3^2 is not the same as $(-3)^2$.

Example 2   *Products with Variable Factors*

a. $-x(-y) = $ ____   Two negative signs

b. $-a(-a) = $ ____   Two negative signs

c. $-9(-a)(-b) = $ _____   Three negative signs

✔ *Checkpoint* **Complete the following exercises.**

1. Find the product $(-1)^5 \cdot (-3)$.	2. Simplify the expression $6(-8t)(-t^2)$.

PROPERTIES OF MULTIPLICATION

Commutative Property The order in which two numbers are multiplied does not change the product.

$a \cdot b = \underline{} \cdot \underline{}$ **Example:** $3 \cdot (-2) = \underline{} \cdot \underline{}$

Associative Property The way you group three numbers when multiplying does not change the product.

$(a \cdot b) \cdot c = \underline{} \cdot (\underline{} \cdot \underline{})$

Example: $(-6 \cdot 2) \cdot 3 = \underline{} \cdot (\underline{} \cdot \underline{})$

Identity Property The product of a number and 1 is the number.

$1 \cdot a = \underline{}$ **Example:** $1 \cdot (-4) = \underline{}$

Property of Zero The product of a number and 0 is 0.

$a \cdot 0 = \underline{}$ **Example:** $(-2) \cdot 0 = \underline{}$

Property of Opposites The product of a number and -1 is the opposite of the number.

$(-1) \cdot a = \underline{}$ **Example:** $(-1) \cdot (-3) = \underline{}$

> Now would be a good time to compare the properties of multiplication to the properties of addition.

Example 3   *Evaluating a Variable Expression*

Evaluate the expression when $x = -3$.

a. $-2x^2$ **b.** $4(-x)^2$

Solution

a. $-2x^2 = -2(\underline{})^2$ **Substitute for x.**

$= -2(\underline{})$ **Evaluate power.**

$= \underline{}$ **Simplify.**

b. $4(-x)^2 = 4[-(\underline{})]^2$ **Substitute for x.**

$= 4(\underline{})^2$ **Simplify power.**

$= 4 \cdot \underline{}$ **Evaluate power.**

$= \underline{}$ **Simplify.**

> Another way to evaluate the expression in Example 3(b) is to simplify the power first, then substitute -3 for x.

2.6 The Distributive Property

Goals • Use the distributive property.
• Simplify expressions by combining like terms.

VOCABULARY

Distributive property

Coefficient

Like terms

Constant terms

Simplified

Example 1 *Using an Area Model*

Find the area of a rectangle whose width is 5 and whose length is $x + 3$.

Solution You can find the area in two ways.

Area of One Rectangle

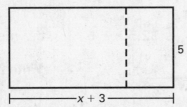

Area of Two Rectangles

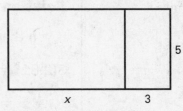

Answer Because both ways produce the same area, the following statement is true.

$$5(\underline{\hspace{2cm}}) = \underline{\hspace{1cm}} + \underline{\hspace{1cm}}$$

THE DISTRIBUTIVE PROPERTY

The product of a and $(b + c)$:

$a(b + c) = ab + \underline{\quad}$ **Example:** $5(x + 2) = \underline{\quad} + \underline{\quad}$

$(b + c)a = \underline{\quad} + ca$ **Example:** $(x + 4)8 = \underline{\quad} + \underline{\quad}$

The product of a and $(b - c)$:

$a(b - c) = \underline{\quad} - ac$ **Example:** $4(x - 7) = \underline{\quad} - \underline{\quad}$

$(b - c)a = ba - \underline{\quad}$ **Example:** $(x - 5)9 = \underline{\quad} - \underline{\quad}$

Example 2   *Using the Distributive Property*

a. $8(x + 9) = \underline{\quad}(\underline{\quad}) + \underline{\quad}(\underline{\quad})$ **Distribute the 8.**

$= \underline{\quad} + \underline{\quad}$ **Simplify.**

b. $-5(x - 6) = \underline{\quad}(\underline{\quad}) - (\underline{\quad})(\underline{\quad})$ **Distribute the −5.**

$= \underline{\quad} - \underline{\quad}$ **Simplify.**

$= \underline{\quad} + \underline{\quad}$

> In Example 2(b) and (c), remember that a factor with a negative sign must multiply *each* term of an expression. Forgetting to distribute the negative sign to each term is a common error.

c. $-x(y - 2x) = \underline{\quad}(\underline{\quad}) - (\underline{\quad})(\underline{\quad})$ **Distribute the −x.**

$= \underline{\quad} - \underline{\quad}$ **Simplify.**

$= \underline{\quad} + \underline{\quad}$

Example 3   *Mental Math Calculations*

Grocery Shopping Cereal is on sale for $2.51 per box. Use the distributive property and mental math to calculate the cost of thr boxes of the cereal.

Solution

If you think of $2.51 as $2.50 + $\underline{\quad}, the mental math is easi

$3(2.51) = 3(2.50 + \underline{\quad})$ **Write 2.51 as a sum.**

$= \underline{\quad}(\underline{\quad}) + \underline{\quad}(\underline{\quad})$ **Use the distributive proper**

$= \underline{\quad} + \underline{\quad}$ **Find the products mentally**

$= \underline{\quad}$ **Find the sum mentally.**

Answer The total cost is $\underline{\quad}$.

Example 4 *Simplifying by Combining Like Terms*

a. $10x + 13x = (\_\_\_ + \_\_\_)x$ Use the distributive property.

    $= \_\_\_$ Add coefficients.

b. $2xy - 5 + 8xy + 3$

$= 2xy + \_\_\_ + 8xy + 3$ Rewrite as an addition expression.

$= 2xy + \_\_\_ + \_\_\_ + 3$ Group like terms.

$= \_\_\_\_\_$ Combine like terms.

c. $9xy + 8y - xy$

$= 9xy + 8y + \_\_\_\_$ Rewrite as an addition expression.

$= 9xy + \_\_\_\_ + \_\_$ Group like terms.

$= \_\_\_\_\_$ Combine like terms.

d. $-x - (3x + x^2)$

$= -x + (\_\_\_)(3x + x^2)$ Rewrite as an addition expression.

$= -x + [(\_\_)(\_\_) + (\_\_)(\_\_)]$ Distribute the ___.

$= -x + (\_\_\_) + (\_\_\_)$ Multiply.

$= \_\_\_ + (\_\_\_)$ Combine like terms.

$= \_\_\_\_\_$ Simplify.

In Example 4(c) and (d), remember that a negative sign preceding a term means that the term is multiplied by negative one.

✔ *Checkpoint* **Complete the following exercises.**

1. Simplify the expression: $-x(4 - x)$.

2. Simplify the expression: $2y^3 + 5y + 4y^3$.

3. Explain how to use the distributive property to mentally find the cost of 8 erasers at $.49 each.

2.7 Division of Real Numbers

Goals • Divide real numbers.
• Use division to simplify algebraic expressions.

VOCABULARY

Reciprocal

DIVISION RULE

To divide a number a by a nonzero number b, multiply a by the reciprocal of b.

$$a \div b = a \cdot \underline{} \qquad \text{Example: } -1 \div 3 = -1 \cdot \underline{} = \underline{}$$

The result is the quotient of a and b.

Example 1 *Dividing Real Numbers*

Find the quotient.

a. $-\dfrac{3}{4} \div \dfrac{5}{12}$ b. $3\dfrac{5}{9} \div 2\dfrac{2}{3}$ c. $\dfrac{5}{2} \div (-25)$ d. $\dfrac{1}{-\dfrac{5}{8}}$

Solution

a. $-\dfrac{3}{4} \div \dfrac{5}{12} = -\dfrac{3}{4} \cdot \underline{} = \underline{} = \underline{}$

b. $3\dfrac{5}{9} \div 2\dfrac{2}{3} = \underline{} \div \underline{} = \underline{} \cdot \underline{} = \underline{} = \underline{}$

c. $\dfrac{5}{2} \div (-25) = \dfrac{5}{2} \div \left(\underline{} \right) = \dfrac{5}{2} \cdot \left(\underline{} \right) = \underline{}$

d. $\dfrac{1}{-\dfrac{5}{8}} = 1 \div \left(-\dfrac{5}{8} \right) = 1 \cdot \left(\underline{} \right) = \underline{} = \underline{}$

> The reciprocal of $-\dfrac{a}{b}$ is $-\dfrac{b}{a}$.
> This is because
> $-\dfrac{a}{b} = \dfrac{-a}{b} = \dfrac{a}{-b}$.

THE SIGN OF A QUOTIENT

- The quotient of two numbers with the same sign is

  _____.

  $$-a \div (-b) = \underline{\quad}$$ Example: $-20 \div (-4) = \underline{\quad}$

- The quotient of two numbers with opposite signs is

  _____.

  $$-a \div b = \underline{\quad}$$ Example: $-20 \div 4 = \underline{\quad}$

Example 2   *Using the Distributive Property to Simplify*

Simplify the expression $\dfrac{56x - 14}{7}$.

$$\frac{56x - 14}{7} = (56x - 14) \div 7$$ **Rewrite fraction as division expression.**

$$= (56x - 14) \cdot \underline{\quad}$$ **Multiply by reciprocal.**

$$= (\underline{\quad})\left(\underline{\quad}\right) - (\underline{\quad})\left(\underline{\quad}\right)$$ **Use distributive property.**

$$= \underline{\quad} - \underline{\quad}$$ **Simplify.**

Example 3   *Evaluating an Expression*

Evaluate the expression when $a = \dfrac{1}{3}$ and $b = -\dfrac{2}{5}$.

a. $-\dfrac{5}{18} \div a$ **b.** $\dfrac{\frac{3}{2}}{\frac{2}{5} + b}$ **c.** $-8 \div b$

Solution

> Remember that can be divided by any nonzero number. The result will always be zero. However, division *by* zero is undefined.

a. $-\dfrac{5}{18} \div a = -\dfrac{5}{18} \div \underline{\quad} = -\dfrac{5}{18} \cdot \underline{\quad} = \underline{\quad}$

b. $\dfrac{\frac{3}{2}}{\frac{2}{5} + b} = \dfrac{\frac{3}{2}}{\frac{2}{5} + \left(\right)} = \dfrac{3}{\cancel{}}$ **(Undefined)**

c. $-8 \div b = -8 \div \left(\right) = -8 \cdot \left(\right) = \underline{\quad}$

Example 4   *Finding the Domain of a Function*

Find the domain of the function $y = \dfrac{3x}{2 + x}$.

Solution

Input some sample values of x.

Input	Substitute	Output
$x = -3$	$\dfrac{3(\boxed{})}{2 + (\boxed{})}$	_____
$x = -2$	$\dfrac{3(\boxed{})}{2 + (\boxed{})}$	_____
$x = -1$	$\dfrac{3(\boxed{})}{2 + (\boxed{})}$	_____
$x = 0$	$\dfrac{3(\boxed{})}{2 + (\boxed{})}$	_____
$x = 1$	$\dfrac{3(\boxed{})}{2 + (\boxed{})}$	_____

Answer From the list, you can see that $x =$ _____ is not in the domain of the function, because you cannot divide by _____. All other real numbers are in the domain because there are no other values of x that will make the denominator zero. The domain is a real numbers *except* $x =$ _____.

✔ *Checkpoint* **Complete the following exercises.**

1. Evaluate the expression $\dfrac{a}{-2b}$ when $a = -\dfrac{1}{5}$ and $b = \dfrac{11}{20}$.	**2.** Find the domain of the function $y = \dfrac{3 - x}{x - 5}$.

2.8 Probability and Odds

Goals • Find the probability of an event.
• Find the odds of an event.

VOCABULARY

Probability of an event

_____

Outcomes

_____

Favorable outcomes

_____

Theoretical probability

_____

Experimental probability

_____

Odds

THE PROBABILITY OF AN EVENT

When all outcomes are _____ , the probability that an
event will occur is given by the formula below.

$$P = \frac{\text{Number of favorable outcomes}}{\text{Total number of outcomes}}$$

Example 1   *Finding the Probability of an Event*

Stuffed Animals A machine randomly selects a stuffed animal. There are 12 giraffes, 3 panda bears, 10 elephants, 5 horses, 21 teddy bears, 4 dogs, and 5 cats. What is the probability *P* that you get an elephant?

Solution

There are ___ + ___ + ___ + ___ + ___ + ___ + ___ = ___ possible outcomes that are equally likely.

$$P = \frac{\text{Number of favorable outcomes}}{\text{Total number of outcomes}} = \frac{\quad}{\quad} = \frac{\quad}{\quad} = \underline{\quad}$$

> The probability in Example 1 is the theoretical probability, because the actual number of favorable outcomes and the total number of outcomes are used.

Example 2   *Using a Survey to Find a Probability*

Surveys Use the circle graph at the right showing the responses of Internet users ages 12 to 17 when asked to name their primary source of research for a school paper or project.

Primary Source of Research

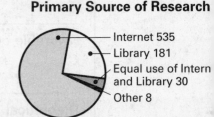

Internet 535
Library 181
Equal use of Intern and Library 30
Other 8

What is the experimental probability that a randomly chosen Internet user in the 12–17-year-old age bracket uses the Internet and the library equally for research projects?

Solution

Let "Equal use of Internet and library" represent the favorable outcomes and "Number surveyed" represent the total number of outcomes.

> The probability in Example 2 is an experimental probability, because it is based on a survey, not the total number of Internet users from ages 12–17.

$$\text{Experimental probability } P = \frac{\text{Equal use of Internet and library}}{\text{Number surveyed}}$$

$$= \frac{\quad}{\quad}$$

$$= \frac{\quad}{\quad} \approx \underline{\quad}$$

Answer The experimental probability that a randomly chosen Internet user in the 12-17-year-old age bracket uses the Internet and the library equally for research projects is about _____ .

THE ODDS OF AN EVENT

When all outcomes are equally likely, the odds that an event will occur are given by the formula below.

$$\text{Odds} = \frac{\text{Number of } \boxed{} \text{ outcomes}}{\text{Number of } \boxed{} \text{ outcomes}}$$

Odds are ways read as the tio of one quantity another. For ample, $\frac{4}{3}$ is read "four to three," t as "four thirds."

Example 3   Finding the Odds of an Event

You randomly choose an integer from 0 through 9. What are the odds that the integer is even?

Solution

There are ___ favorable outcomes: _____ .
There are ___ unfavorable outcomes: _____ .

$$\text{Odds} = \frac{\text{Number of favorable outcomes}}{\text{Number of unfavorable outcomes}} = \frac{}{} = \frac{}{}$$

Answer The odds that the integer is even are ___ to ___ .

Example 4   Finding Odds from Probability

For a randomly selected U.S. trip of at least 100 miles, the probability that the principal means of transportation is a personal use vehicle is $\frac{77}{100}$. Find the odds in favor of a personal use vehicle being the principal means of transportation.

Solution

The phrase − (Probability ent will occur)" is e probability that e event will not ccur.

$$\text{Odds} = \frac{\text{Probability event will occur}}{1 - (\text{Probability event will occur})}$$

$$= \frac{\boxed{}}{1 - \boxed{}} \qquad \text{Substitute for probabilities.}$$

$$= \frac{}{} \qquad \text{Simplify denominator.}$$

$$= \frac{}{} \qquad \text{Multiply numerator and denominator by 100.}$$

Answer The odds that a personal use vehicle is the principal means of transportation are ____ to ____ .

✓ *Checkpoint* **Complete the following exercises.**

1. The results of rolling a six-sided number cube 100 times are: 1–10; 2–17; 3–15; 4–20; 5–14; 6–24. Use these results to find the experimental probability of rolling a 3. Then find the theoretical probability.

2. Find the odds in favor of rolling a 3 on a six-sided number cube.

3. The probability that it will rain today is 0.30. What are the odds that it will rain today

Words to Review

Give an example of each vocabulary word.

Real numbers	Integers
Absolute value	Counterexample
Matrix	Distributive property
Like terms	Reciprocal
Probability of an event	Odds

Review your notes and Chapter 2 by using the Chapter Review on pages 122–124 of your textbook.

3.1 Solving Equations Using Addition and Subtraction

Goals • Solve linear equations using addition and subtraction.
• Use linear equations to solve real-life problems.

VOCABULARY

Equivalent equations

Inverse operations

Solution step

Linear equation

TRANSFORMATIONS THAT PRODUCE EQUIVALENT EQUATION

	Original Equation		Equivale Equatio
• Add the same number to *each* side.	$x - 3 = 5$	**Add** ___.	$x =$ _
• Subtract the same number from *each* side.	$x + 6 = 10$	**Subtract** ___.	$x =$ _
• Simplify one or both sides.	$x = 8 - 3$	**Simplify.**	$x =$ _
• Interchange the sides.	$7 = x$	**Interchange.**	$x =$ _

Example 1 *Adding to Each Side*

Solve $x - 9 = -20$.

On the left side of the equation, 9 is subtracted from x. To isolate x, you need to undo the subtraction by applying the inverse operation of adding ___ . Remember that you need to add ___ to *each* side.

$$x - 9 = -20 \qquad \text{Write original equation.}$$

$$x - 9 + \underline{} = -20 + \underline{} \qquad \text{Add \underline{} to each side.}$$

$$x = \underline{} \qquad \text{Simplify.}$$

Answer The solution is _____ .

> You can check
> ~~y~~ r solution by
> ~~su~~ bstituting your
> ~~sol~~ ution for x in the
> ~~ori~~ ginal equation.

Example 2 *Simplifying First*

Solve $n - (-8) = -2$.

$$n - (-8) = -2 \qquad \text{Write original equation.}$$

$$n + 8 = -2 \qquad \text{Simplify.}$$

$$n + 8 - \underline{} = -2 - \underline{} \qquad \text{Subtract \underline{} from each side.}$$

$$n = \underline{} \qquad \text{Simplify.}$$

✔ **Checkpoint** Solve the equation. Check your solution in the original equation.

1. $x - 7 = -15$	**2.** $n - (-6) = 4$	**3.** $-7 = 10 + y$
4. $5 - (-z) = 21$	**5.** $m - \lvert -3 \rvert = 14$	**6.** $-8 = -b + (-2)$

3.2 Solving Equations Using Multiplication and Division

Goals • Solve linear equations using multiplication and division.
• Use multiplication and division equations to solve problem

VOCABULARY

Properties of equality

Ratio of *a* to *b*

Similar triangles

TRANSFORMATIONS THAT PRODUCE EQUIVALENT EQUATIONS

	Original Equation		Equivalent Equation
• Multiply each side of the equation by the same nonzero number.	$\dfrac{x}{2} = 3$	**Multiply by** ___ .	$x =$ ___
• Divide each side of the equation by the same nonzero number.	$4x = 12$	**Divide by** ___ .	$x =$ ___

Example 1 — *Dividing Each Side of an Equation*

Solve $8x = -3$.

Solution

On the left side of the equation, x is multiplied by 8. To isolate x, you need to undo the multiplication by applying the inverse operation of dividing by ___ .

$$8x = -3 \qquad \text{Write original equation.}$$

$$\frac{8x}{\square} = \frac{-3}{\square} \qquad \text{Divide each side by ___.}$$

$$x = \underline{\hspace{2cm}} \qquad \text{Simplify.}$$

Example 2 — *Multiplying Each Side of an Equation*

Solve $\dfrac{x}{-3} = 60$.

Solution

On the left side of the equation, x is divided by -3. You can isolate x by multiplying each side by ____ to undo the division.

$$\frac{x}{-3} = 60 \qquad \text{Write original equation.}$$

$$\underline{\hspace{1.5cm}}\left(\frac{x}{-3}\right) = \underline{\hspace{1cm}}(60) \qquad \text{Multiply each side by ___.}$$

$$x = \underline{\hspace{1.5cm}} \qquad \text{Simplify.}$$

Example 3 — *Multiplying Each Side by a Reciprocal*

> To isolate the variable, multiply the fractional coefficient by its reciprocal.

$$-\frac{3}{4}m = 15 \qquad \text{Write original equation.}$$

$$\underline{\hspace{1.5cm}}\left(-\frac{3}{4}m\right) = \underline{\hspace{1.5cm}}\,15 \qquad \text{Multiply each side by} \underline{\hspace{1.5cm}}.$$

$$m = \underline{\hspace{1cm}} \qquad \text{Simplify.}$$

PROPERTIES OF EQUALITY

Addition Property of Equality If $a = b$, then $\underline{} + c = \underline{} + c$.

Subtraction Property of Equality If $a = b$, then $\underline{} - c = \underline{} - c$.

Multiplication Property of Equality If $a = b$, then $c\underline{} = c\underline{}$.

Division Property of Equality If $a = b$ and $c \neq 0$, then

$$\frac{\underline{}}{\underline{}} = \frac{\underline{}}{\underline{}}.$$

✔ *Checkpoint* **Solve the equation.**

1. $9x = 72$	**2.** $4 = 11m$	**3.** $\dfrac{y}{-6} = -15$
4. $-\dfrac{5}{2} = \dfrac{n}{2}$	**5.** $-\dfrac{2}{9}b = 18$	**6.** $\dfrac{3}{35} = \dfrac{2}{5}a$

3.3 Solving Multi-Step Equations

Goals • Use two or more transformations to solve an equation.
• Use multi-step equations to solve real-life problems.

Example 1   *Solving a Linear Equation*

Solve $\frac{1}{2}x - 7 = -10$.

To isolate the variable, undo the _____ and then the

_____.

$$\frac{1}{2}x - 7 = -10 \qquad \text{Write original equation.}$$

$$\frac{1}{2}x - 7 + \underline{\ \ } = -10 + \underline{\ \ } \qquad \text{Add ___ to each side.}$$

$$\frac{1}{2}x = \underline{\ \ \ \ } \qquad \text{Simplify.}$$

$$\underline{\ \ }\left(\frac{1}{2}x\right) = \underline{\ \ }(\underline{\ \ }) \qquad \text{Multiply each side by ___ .}$$

$$x = \underline{\ \ \ \ } \qquad \text{Simplify.}$$

Example 2   *Combining Like Terms First*

Solve $8x - 5x + 16 = -29$.

Solution

$$8x - 5x + 16 = -29 \qquad \text{Write original equation.}$$

$$\underline{\ \ \ \ } + 16 = -29 \qquad \text{Combine like terms.}$$

$$\underline{\ \ \ \ } + 16 - \underline{\ \ \ } = -29 - \underline{\ \ \ } \qquad \text{Subtract ____ from each side.}$$

$$\underline{\ \ \ } = \underline{\ \ \ \ } \qquad \text{Simplify.}$$

$$\frac{\underline{\ \ \ }}{\underline{\ \ \ }} = \frac{}{\underline{\ \ \ \ \ }} \qquad \text{Divide each side by ___ .}$$

$$x = \underline{\ \ \ \ } \qquad \text{Simplify.}$$

Example 3   *Using the Distributive Property*

Solve $9x - 5(x + 6) = -10$.

Solution

| **Method 1** | **Method 2** |
| Show All Steps | Do Some Steps Mentally |

$$9x - 5(x + 6) = -10 \qquad\qquad 9x - 5(x + 6) = -10$$

$$9x - \underline{\hspace{1.5cm}} = -10 \qquad\qquad 9x - \underline{\hspace{1.5cm}} = -10$$

$$\underline{\hspace{1.5cm}} = -10 \qquad\qquad \underline{\hspace{1.5cm}} = -10$$

$$\underline{\hspace{2cm}} = -10 \; \underline{\hspace{0.8cm}} \qquad\qquad \underline{\hspace{0.6cm}} = \underline{\hspace{0.6cm}}$$

$$\frac{\underline{\hspace{0.6cm}}}{} = \frac{\underline{\hspace{0.6cm}}}{} \qquad\qquad\qquad x = \underline{\hspace{0.6cm}}$$

$$\frac{\underline{\hspace{1cm}}}{} = \frac{\underline{\hspace{1cm}}}{}$$

$$x = \underline{\hspace{0.6cm}}$$

Example 4   *Multiplying by a Reciprocal First*

Solve $24 = \dfrac{3}{4}(x + 7)$.

Solution

It is easier to solve this equation if you don't distribute $\dfrac{3}{4}$.

$$24 = \frac{3}{4}(x + 7) \qquad\qquad \text{Write original equation.}$$

$$24 = \underline{\hspace{1cm}}\left(\frac{3}{4}\right)(x + 7) \qquad \text{Multiply by reciprocal of } \underline{\hspace{0.6cm}}.$$

$$\underline{\hspace{1cm}} \; \underline{\hspace{1cm}}$$

$$\underline{\hspace{0.6cm}} = \underline{\hspace{1cm}} \qquad\qquad\qquad \text{Simplify.}$$

$$\underline{\hspace{0.6cm}} = x \qquad\qquad\qquad \text{Subtract } \underline{\hspace{0.5cm}} \text{ from each side.}$$

✓ *Checkpoint* **Solve the equation.**

1. $3 - 4x = 19$	**2.** $40 = 29 + \dfrac{1}{3}x$	**3.** $7(x - 1) = 49$
4. $-2(3 - x) = 30$	**5.** $\dfrac{2}{5}(x + 23) = 8$	**6.** $16 = -\dfrac{4}{7}(x - 19)$
7. $\dfrac{3}{2}x + x = -15$	**8.** $\dfrac{5x}{2} + 10 = 15$	**9.** $-6 = 10 - \dfrac{x}{3}$

Solving Equations with Variables on Both Sides

Goals • Collect variables on one side of an equation.
• Use equations to solve real-life problems.

VOCABULARY

Identity

Example 1   *Collect Variables on One Side*

Solve $4x - 10 = 32 - 3x$.

Solution

Look at the coefficients of the *x*-terms. Because 4 is greater than -3, collect the *x*-terms on the left side.

$4x - 10 = 32 - 3x$	Write original equation.
$4x - 10 + \underline{} = 32 - 3x + \underline{}$	Add ____ to each side.
$\underline{} - 10 = 32$	Simplify.
$\underline{} - 10 + \underline{} = 32 + \underline{}$	Add ____ to each side.
$\underline{} = \underline{}$	Simplify.
$\dfrac{\underline{}}{\underline{}} = \dfrac{\underline{}}{\underline{}}$	Divide each side by ___ .
$x = \underline{}$	Simplify.
Check $4x - 10 = 32 - 3x$	Write original equation.
$4(\underline{}) - 10 \overset{?}{=} 32 - 3(\underline{})$	Substitute ___ for *x*.
$\underline{} = \underline{}$	Solution is _____ .

Example 2 *Many Solutions or No Solution*

Solve the equation.

a. $2(4x + 5) = 8x + 10$ **b.** $x - 1 = x + 7$

Solution

a. $2(4x + 5) = 8x + 10$ Write original equation.

   _____ $= 8x + 10$ Use distributive property.

    ___ $=$ ___   Subtract ____ from each side.

Answer All values of x _____ , because _____
_____ . The original equation is _____ .

b. $x - 1 = x + 7$ Write original equation.

   _____   Subtract ___ from each side.

Answer The original equation _____ , because
_____ .

Example 3 *Solving More Complicated Equations*

Solve $3(2 - x) + 2x = -5(x + 2)$.

Solution

$3(2 - x) + 2x = -5(x + 2)$ Write original equation.

_____ $+ 2x =$ _____   Use distributive property.

  _____ $=$ _____   Combine like terms.

  _____ $=$ ____   Add ____ to each side.

  ____ $=$ _____   Subtract ___ from each side.

    $x =$ ____   Divide each side by ___ .

✅ *Checkpoint* **Solve the equation.**

1. $6x + 33 = 5x$	**2.** $10y + 22 = 8y$
3. $b = 9b - 24$	**4.** $-2n = 3n + 17$
5. $13m - 26 = 13m$	**6.** $-6(4 - 2x) = 12x - 24$
7. $15a - 2(4a + 5) = -6a$	**8.** $\frac{1}{4}(12 - 16q) = 5(q + 6)$

3.5 Linear Equations and Problem Solving

Goals • Draw a diagram to help you understand real-life problems.
• Use tables and graphs to check your answers.

Example 1 *Visualizing a Problem*

Dog Pen You have 112 feet of fencing to enclose a rectangular pen for your dog. To provide sufficient running space for the dog to exercise, the pen is to be three times as long as it is wide. Find the dimensions of the pen.

Solution

Draw a Diagram The diagram of the pen shows that the length is three times the width. To find the dimensions of the pen, use the formula for the perimeter of a rectangle.

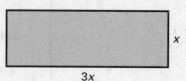

Verbal Model							
Perimeter	= 2 ·	Width	+ 2 ·	Length			

Labels   Perimeter = _____   (feet)
          Width = ___   (feet)
          Length = _____   (feet)

Algebraic Model   ____ = 2 · ___ + 2 · ____   **Write algebraic model.**
          ____ = ___ + ____   **Simplify.**
          ____ = ____   **Combine like terms.**
          ____ = x **Divide each side by ___ .**

Answer The width of the pen is _____ and the length of the pen is 3(____), or _____ .

Example 2 *Using a Graph as a Check*

Savings Sara and Jim both decide to save some money each week. Sara has already saved $100, and she plans to save $10 a week. Jim plans to save $15 a week. In how many weeks will Jim and Sara have saved the same amount?

Solution

First write an expression for the amount of money Sara has saved. Then set this expression equal to the expression for the amount of money that Jim has saved.

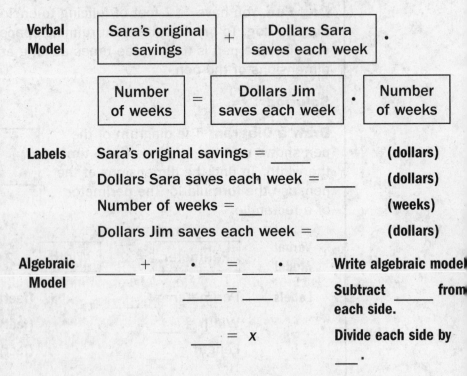

Verbal Model

| Sara's original savings | + | Dollars Sara saves each week | • |

| Number of weeks | = | Dollars Jim saves each week | • | Number of weeks |

Labels   Sara's original savings = _____   (dollars)

Dollars Sara saves each week = ____   (dollars)

Number of weeks = ____   (weeks)

Dollars Jim saves each week = ____   (dollars)

Algebraic Model

____ + ____ • ____ = ____ • ____   Write algebraic model

____ = ____   Subtract _____ from each side.

____ = x   Divide each side by ____ .

Answer Sara and Jim will have saved the same amount after ____ weeks.

Check Use a graph to check your answer. Make a table and plot the points.

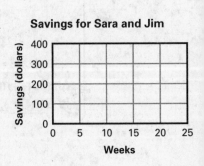

Savings for Sara and Jim

1. You have 78 feet of fencing to enclose a rectangular pen for your rabbit. To provide sufficient space for the rabbit to exercise, the pen is to be twice as long as it is wide. Find the dimensions of the pen.

---

2. You and your brother are painting a room. You are painting at a rate of 12 square feet per minute and your brother is painting at a rate of 16 square feet per minute. When your brother started painting, you had already painted 40 square feet. In how many minutes will you and your brother have painted the same amount? Use a table or graph to check your work.

3.6 Solving Decimal Equations

Goals • Find exact and approximate solutions of equations that contain decimals.
• Solve real-life problems that use decimals.

VOCABULARY

Round-off error

Example 1   *Rounding for the Final Answer*

Solve $-48x + 31 = 124$. Round to the nearest hundredth.

$-48x + 31 = 124$	Write original equation.
$-48x = \underline{\quad}$	Subtract ___ from each side.
$x = \dfrac{\quad}{\quad}$	Divide each side by ___ .
$x = \underline{\qquad}$	Use a calculator.
$x \approx \underline{\qquad}$	Round to nearest hundredth.

Answer The solution is approximately _____ .

Check When you substitute a rounded answer into the original equation, the two sides of the equation may not be exactly equal, but they should be almost equal.

$-48x + 31 = 124$	Write original equation.
$-48(\underline{\quad}) + 31 \overset{?}{=} 124$	Substitute _____ for x.
$\underline{\quad} \approx 124$	Is the answer reasonable? ___

Example 2 *Original Equation Involving Decimals*

Solve $2.53x - 60.17 = 0.38x + 5.48$. Round to the nearest hundredth.

Use the same methods you learned for solving equations without decimals.

$2.53x - 60.17 = 0.38x + 5.48$	**Write original equation.**
$\underline{\hspace{1.5cm}} - 60.17 = 5.48$	**Subtract** $\underline{\hspace{1cm}}$ **from each side.**
$\underline{\hspace{1.5cm}} = \underline{\hspace{1.5cm}}$	**Add** $\underline{\hspace{1cm}}$ **to each side.**
$x = \dfrac{\underline{\hspace{1.5cm}}}{\underline{\hspace{1cm}}}$	**Divide each side by** $\underline{\hspace{1cm}}$.
$x \approx \underline{\hspace{2cm}}$	**Use a calculator.**
$x \approx \underline{\hspace{1.5cm}}$	**Round to nearest hundredth.**

Answer The solution is approximately $\underline{\hspace{1.5cm}}$. Check this in the original equation.

✔ *Checkpoint* **Solve the equation. Round to the nearest hundredth.**

1. $11x - 5 = 26$	**2.** $23 - 6y = 7$	**3.** $-48 = 13n + 14$

4. $6.26x - 54.89 = 0.86x + 9.76$

5. $12.78 + 2.75x = 5.26 + 7.23x$

Example 3   *Changing Decimal Coefficients to Integers*

Solve $3.7 - 8.4x = 1.2x + 35.9$. Round to the nearest tenth.

Solution

> Because the coefficients and constant terms each have only one decimal place, you can rewrite the equation without decimals by multiplying each side by 10.

$$3.7 - 8.4x = 1.2x + 35.9$$ Write original equation.

$$37 - 84x = 12x + 359$$ Multiply each side by 10.

$$37 = \underline{\quad\quad} + 359$$ Add _____ to each side.

$$\underline{\quad\quad} = \underline{\quad\quad}$$ Subtract _____ from each side

$$\underline{\quad\quad} = x$$ Divide each side by ____.

$$\underline{\quad\quad} \approx x$$ Use a calculator.

$$\underline{\quad\quad} \approx x$$ Round to nearest tenth.

Answer The solution is approximately _____. Check this in the original equation.

✔ *Checkpoint* **Multiply the equation by a power of 10 to write an equivalent equation with integer coefficients.**

6. $7.2x + 1.3 = 3.8 + 4.2x$	**7.** $0.97y - 0.29 = 0.83y$

Solve the equation. Round to the nearest hundredth.

8. $37.2x + 95.2 = 79.9x$	**9.** $56.44y + 28.03 =$ $75.67y - 81.97$

Formulas and Functions

Goals
- Solve a formula for one of its variables.
- Rewrite an equation in function form.

VOCABULARY

Formula

Example 1   *Solving an Area Formula*

Use the formula for the area of a rectangle, $A = \ell w$. Find a formula for w in terms of A and ℓ.

Solve for width w.

$A = \ell w$ Write original formula.

$\underline{\quad} = w$ To isolate ____ , divide each side by ___ .

Example 2   *Solving a Temperature Conversion Formula*

Solve the temperature formula $F = \dfrac{9}{5}C + 32$ for C.

$$F = \frac{9}{5}C + 32$$ Write original formula.

$$F - \underline{\quad} = \frac{9}{5}C + 32 - \underline{\quad}$$ Subtract ____ from each side.

$$F - \underline{\quad} = \frac{9}{5}C$$ Simplify.

$$\underline{\quad} \cdot (F - \underline{\quad}) = \underline{\quad} \cdot \frac{9}{5}C$$ Multiply each side by ___ .

$$\underline{\quad}(F - \underline{\quad}) = C$$ Simplify.

✔ Checkpoint Solve for the indicated variable.

1. Solve for ℓ: $P = 2\ell + 2w$	**2.** Solve for w: $V = \ell wh$	**3.** Solve for r: $C = 2\pi r$

4. The distance d traveled for a rate r and time t is given by $d = rt$. Solve this formula for r. Then use the formula to find the speed of a car that takes 8 hours to drive 400 miles.

Example 3 *Rewriting an Equation in Function Form*

Rewrite the equation $-4x + y = 7$ so that y is a function of x.

$\qquad -4x + y = 7 \qquad\qquad$ Write original equation.

$-4x + y + \underline{\quad} = 7 + \underline{\quad} \qquad$ Add $\underline{\quad}$ to each side.

$\qquad\qquad y = 7 + \underline{\quad} \qquad\qquad$ Simplify.

Answer The equation $\underline{\qquad\qquad}$ represents $\underline{\quad}$ as a function of $\underline{\quad}$.

✔ Checkpoint Rewrite the equation so that y is a function of x.

5. $16x + y = -11$	**6.** $15 = 2x - y$	**7.** $9 - y = 3x$

3.8 Rates, Ratios, and Percents

Goals
- Use rates and ratios to model and solve real-life problems.
- Use percents to model and solve real-life problems.

VOCABULARY

Rate of *a* per *b*

Unit rate

Example 1 *Interpreting Large Numbers*

Beverage Consumption How can you relate this information to individual consumption?

Estimated Consumption of Selected Beverages in the U.S. in a Recent Year		
Milk	**Bottled water**	**Fruit juice**
6306 million gallons	4832 million gallons	2539 million gallons

Solution

One solution is to find the average rate of consumption *per person* so that people can compare themselves to the average. You can do this by dividing by the total population, which for this year was about 273 million.

Milk: about ____ gallons per person

Bottled water: about ____ gallons per person

Fruit juice: about ____ gallons per person

Example 2 *Using Collected Data*

Pets You have recorded the distance you walk your dog every day and the time each walk takes. Estimate the speed at which you walk your dog.

Miles	1.5	1.5	1.75	1.25
Hours	0.4	0.3	0.5	0.3

Solution

It took you a total of _____ hours to walk a total of ___ miles. Let x represent your walking speed. To estimate x, you can solve the following equation.

$$\text{Distance} \rightarrow \underline{\quad} = x \cdot \underline{\quad} \leftarrow \text{Time}$$

Answer The solution is $x = $ ___ , so your walking speed is about ___ miles per hour.

Example 3 *Applying Unit Analysis*

Exchanging Money You are visiting Canada and you want to exchange $125 for Canadian dollars. The rate of currency exchange is 1.48 Canadian dollars per United States dollar. How many Canadian dollars will you receive?

Solution

Unit Analysis You can use unit analysis to write an equation.

$$\text{U.S. dollars} \cdot \frac{\underline{\qquad}}{\underline{\qquad}} = \text{Canadian dollars}$$

$$D \cdot \frac{\underline{\qquad}}{\underline{\qquad}} = C \qquad \text{Write equation.}$$

$$\underline{\qquad} \cdot \frac{\underline{\qquad}}{\underline{\qquad}} = C \qquad \text{Substitute } \underline{\qquad} \text{ for}$$

$$\underline{\qquad} = C \qquad \text{Simplify.}$$

Answer You will receive _____ Canadian dollars.

Example 4 *Finding Percents*

Movies In a survey of 950 students, what percent of respondents said that their favorite type of movie is a comedy?

Movie Type	Students
Drama	181
Comedy	439
Action	239
Other	91

Solution

To find the percent, divide the number of students who prefer to watch comedies by the number of students surveyed. Then write the result as a _____ .

$$\frac{\boxed{}}{950} = \underline{\hspace{4cm}} \approx \underline{\hspace{1cm}} \%$$

Answer About _____ of students surveyed prefer to watch comedies.

✔ *Checkpoint* **Complete the following exercises.**

1. An amusement park is open 330 days per year and received 3,600,000 visitors. Find the number of visitors per day. Round your answer to the nearest whole number.

_____

2. In Example 3, suppose you want to exchange $250 for Canadian dollars. How many Canadian dollars will you receive?

_____

3. In Example 4, what percent of respondents said that their favorite type of movie is a drama?

Words to Review

Give an example of the vocabulary word.

Equivalent equations	Inverse operations
Solution step	Linear equation
Property of equality	Ratio of *a* to *b*
Identity	Formula
Rate of *a* per *b*	Unit rate

Review your notes and Chapter 3 by using the Chapter Review on pages 190–192 of your textbook.

4.1 Coordinates and Scatter Plots

Goals • Plot points in a coordinate plane.
• Draw a scatter plot and make predictions about real-life situations.

VOCABULARY

Coordinate plane

Ordered pair

---

x-coordinate

---

y-coordinate

Graph

Scatter plot

Example 1 — *Plotting Points in a Coordinate Plane*

Plot the points $A(-2, 3)$, $B(3, -4)$, and $C(0, -2)$ in a coordinate plane.

Solution

To plot the point $A(-2, 3)$, start at the _____ . Move ___ units to the _____ and ___ units ____ .

To plot the point $B(3, -4)$, start at the _____ . Move ___ units to the _____ and ___ units _____ .

To plot the point $C(0, -2)$, start at the _____ . Move ___ units to the _____ and ___ units _____ .

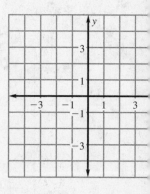

✓ **Checkpoint** Plot the points on the same coordinate plane.

1. $A(-3, -2)$ **2.** $B(4, 0)$ **3.** $C(1, 4)$ **4.** $D(-3, 2)$

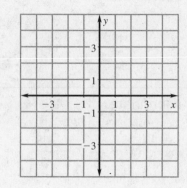

Example 2 *Making a Scatter Plot*

NCAA Basketball Teams The number of NCAA men's college basketball teams is shown in the table.

Year	1995	1996	1997	1998	1999	2000
Teams	868	866	865	895	926	932

a. Draw a scatter plot of the data.

b. Describe the pattern of the number of men's basketball teams.

Solution

a. Let M represent _____. Let t represent
_____.

Because you want to see how the number of teams changed over time, put t on the _____ axis and M on the _____ axis.

Choose a scale. Use a break in the scale for the number of teams to focus on values between _____ and _____ .

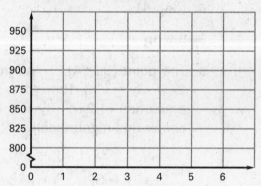

NCAA Men's Basketball Teams

b. From the scatter plot, you can see that the number of men's basketball teams in the NCAA was _____ for three years and then began to _____ .

4.2 Graphing Linear Equations

Goals
- Graph a linear equation using a table or a list of values.
- Graph horizontal and vertical lines.

VOCABULARY

Solution of an equation

Graph of an equation

Example 1   *Verifying Solutions of an Equation*

Use the graph to decide whether the point lies on the graph of $2x + 3y = -6$. Justify your answer algebraically.

a. $(3, -4)$ **b.** $(-4, 1)$

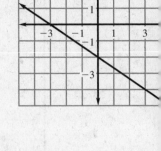

Solution

a. The point $(3, -4)$ ___ on the graph of $2x + 3y = -6$. Therefore, $(3, -4)$ ___ a solution of $2x + 3y = -6$. You can check this algebraically.

$$2x + 3y = -6 \qquad \text{Write original equation.}$$
$$2(\underline{}) + 3(\underline{}) \overset{?}{=} -6 \qquad \text{Substitute ___ for } x \text{ and ___ for}$$
$$\underline{}\ \underline{}\ -6 \qquad \text{Simplify. _____ statement.}$$

b. The point $(-4, 1)$ _____ on the graph of $2x + 3y = -6$. Therefore, $(-4, 1)$ _____ a solution. You can check this algebraically.

$$2x + 3y = -6 \qquad \text{Write original equation.}$$
$$2(\underline{}) + 3(\underline{}) = -6 \qquad \text{Substitute ____ for } x \text{ and __ for}$$
$$\underline{}\ \underline{}\ -6 \qquad \text{Simplify. _____ statement}$$

GRAPHING A LINEAR EQUATION

Step 1 Rewrite the equation in _____, if necessary.

Step 2 Choose a few values of ___ and make a _____.

Step 3 Plot the points from the table of values. A line through these points is the _____ of the equation.

Example 2   Graphing an Equation

Use a table of values to graph the equation $x + 4y = 4$.

1. Rewrite the equation in function form by solving for y.

$x + 4y = 4$	**Write original equation.**
$4y = $ _____	**Subtract ___ from each side.**
$y = $ _____	**Divide each side by ___.**

After an equation is rewritten in function form, it is easier to make a table of values.

2. Choose a few values of x and make a table of values.

Choose x.	−4	0	4
Evaluate y.			

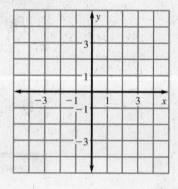

The solutions are

$(-4,$ __$), (0,$ __$),$ and $(4,$ __$).$

3. Plot the points and draw a line through them.

✔ *Checkpoint* **Complete the following exercise.**

1. Use a table of values to graph the equation $x - 2y = 1$.

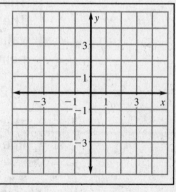

EQUATIONS OF HORIZONTAL AND VERTICAL LINES

In the coordinate plane, the graph of $y = b$ is a _____ line.

In the coordinate plane, the graph of $x = a$ is a _____ line.

Example 3   *Graphing y = b*

Graph the equation $y = -3$.

Solution

The equation does not have x as a variable. The y-value is always -3, regardless of the value of x. For instance, here are some points that are solutions of the equation:

    $(-3, -3), (0, -3), (3, -3)$.

The graph of the equation is a _____ line ___ units _____ the x-axis.

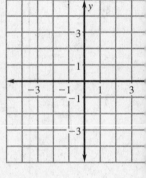

Example 4   *Graphing x = a*

Graph the equation $x = 2$.

Solution

The equation does not have y as a variable. The x-value is always 2, regardless of the value of y. For instance, here are some points that are solutions of the equation:

    $(2, -3), (2, 0), (2, 3)$.

The graph of the equation is a _____ line ___ units to the _____ of the y-axis.

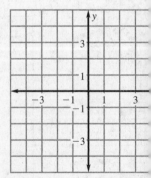

Quick Graphs Using Intercepts

• Find the intercepts of the graph of a linear equation.
• Use intercepts to make a quick graph of a linear equation.

VOCABULARY

x-intercept

y-intercept

Example 1 *Finding Intercepts*

Find the *x*-intercept and the *y*-intercept of the graph of the equation $-3x + 4y = 12$.

1. To find the *x*-intercept of $-3x + 4y = 12$, let $y = \underline{\quad}$.

$$-3x + 4y = 12 \qquad \text{Write original equation.}$$

$$-3x + 4(\underline{\quad}) = 12 \qquad \text{Substitute } \underline{\quad} \text{ for } y.$$

$$\underline{\qquad} = 12 \qquad \text{Simplify.}$$

$$x = \underline{\quad} \qquad \text{Solve for } x.$$

The *x*-intercept is $\underline{\quad}$. The line crosses the *x*-axis at the point $(\underline{\quad}, \underline{\quad})$.

2. To find the *y*-intercept of $-3x + 4y = 12$, let $x = \underline{\quad}$.

$$-3x + 4y = 12 \qquad \text{Write original equation.}$$

$$-3(\underline{\quad}) + 4y = 12 \qquad \text{Substitute } \underline{\quad} \text{ for } x.$$

$$\underline{\quad} = 12 \qquad \text{Simplify.}$$

$$y = \underline{\quad} \qquad \text{Solve for } y.$$

The *y*-intercept is $\underline{\quad}$. The line crosses the *y*-axis at the point $(\underline{\quad}, \underline{\quad})$.

Example 2 **Making a Quick Graph**

Graph the equation $3x + 2.5y = 7.5$.

Solution

Find the *x*-intercept.

$3x + 2.5y = 7.5$	Write original equation.
$3x + 2.5(\underline{}) = 7.5$	Substitute ___ for *y*.
$\underline{} = 7.5$	Simplify.
$x = \underline{}$	Solve for *x*. The *x*-intercept is ___

Find the *y*-intercept.

$3x + 2.5y = 7.5$	Write original equation.
$3(\underline{}) + 2.5y = 7.5$	Substitute ___ for *x*.
$\underline{} = 7.5$	Simplify.
$y = \underline{}$	Solve for *y*. The *y*-intercept is ___ .

> Only two points are needed to determine a line.

Plot the points (____ , 0) and (0, ___) and draw a _____ through them.

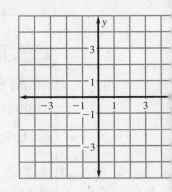

✔ **Checkpoint** **Complete the following exercise.**

1. Find the *x*-intercept and the *y*-intercept of the graph of the equation $-4x + 5y = 20$. Then graph the equation.

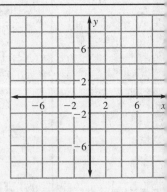

Example 3 *Drawing Appropriate Scales*

Graph the equation $y = 5x + 35$.

Find the intercepts by substituting ___ for y and then ___ for x.

$$y = 5x + 35$$
$$\_\_ = 5x + 35$$
$$\_\_\_\_ = 5x$$
$$\_\_\_\_ = x$$

The x-intercept is _____ .

$$y = 5x + 35$$
$$y = 5(\_\_) + 35$$
$$y = \_\_\_$$

The y-intercept is ___ .

Draw a coordinate plane that includes the points (_____ , ___) and (__ , _____). With these values, it is reasonable to use tick marks at 7-unit intervals.

> When making a quick graph, find the intercepts before drawing the coordinate plane. This will help you find an appropriate scale on each axis.

You may want to draw axes with at least two tick marks to the left of -7 and to the right of 0 on the x-axis and two tick marks below 0 and above 35 on the y-axis.

Plot the points (_____ , ___) and (__ , _____) and draw a line through them.

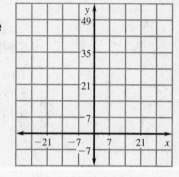

✔ *Checkpoint* **Complete the following exercise.**

2. Graph the equation $y = -5x + 50$.

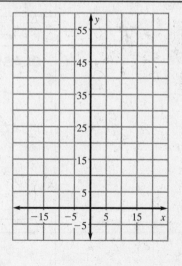

4.4 The Slope of a Line

Goals • Find the slope of a line using two of its points.
• Interpret slope as a rate of change in real-life situations.

VOCABULARY

Slope

_____

Rate of change

FINDING THE SLOPE OF A LINE

The slope m of the nonvertical line
passing through the point (x_1, y_1)
and (x_2, y_2) is

$$m = \frac{\text{rise}}{\text{run}} = \frac{\text{change in } \boxed{}}{\text{change in } \boxed{}}$$

$$= \frac{\boxed{}}{\boxed{}}$$

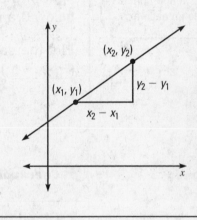

CLASSIFICATION OF LINES BY SLOPE

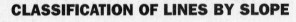

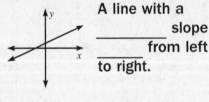
A line with a
_____ slope
_____ from left
to right.

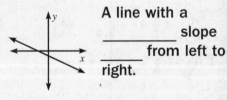
A line with a
_____ slope
_____ from left to
right.

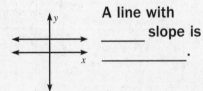
A line with
_____ slope is
_____.

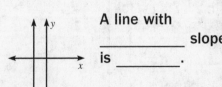
A line with
_____ slope
is _____.

Example 1 *Finding the Slope of a Line*

Find the slope of the line passing through the points. Then classify the line by its slope.

a. $(-2, -3), (1, 2)$ **b.** $(-2, -3), (4, -3)$ **c.** $(-1, -4), (-1, -2)$

Solution

a. Let $(x_1, y_1) = (\underline{\quad}, \underline{\quad})$ and $(x_2, y_2) = (\underline{\quad}, \underline{\quad})$.

$$m = \frac{y_2 - y_1}{x_2 - x_1}$$ Formula for slope.

$= \underline{\qquad\qquad}$ Substitute values.

$= \underline{\qquad\qquad}$ Simplify.

The slope of the line is _____ , so the line _____ from left to right.

b. Let $(x_1, y_1) = (\underline{\quad}, \underline{\quad})$ and $(x_2, y_2) = (\underline{\quad}, \underline{\quad})$.

$$m = \frac{y_2 - y_1}{x_2 - x_1}$$ Formula for slope.

$= \underline{\qquad\qquad}$ Substitute values.

$= \underline{\qquad\qquad}$ Simplify.

The slope of the line is _____ , so the line is _____ .

c. Let $(x_1, y_1) = (\underline{\quad}, \underline{\quad})$ and $(x_2, y_2) = (\underline{\quad}, \underline{\quad})$.

$$m = \frac{y_2 - y_1}{x_2 - x_1}$$ Formula for slope.

$= \underline{\qquad\qquad}$ Substitute values.

$= \underline{\qquad\qquad}$ Simplify.

The slope of the line is _____ , so the line is _____ .

Checkpoint Find the slope of the line passing through the points. Then classify the line by its slope.

1. $(-5, 2), (4, -1)$	**2.** $(6, 2), (9, 2)$
3. $(-7, 0), (-7, 8)$	**4.** $(2, -4), (8, 6)$

Direct Variation

Goals • Write linear equations that represent direct variation.
• Use a ratio to write an equation for direct variation.

VOCABULARY

Constant of variation

Direct variation

PROPERTIES OF GRAPHS OF DIRECT VARIATION MODELS

• The graph of $y = kx$ is a
  line through the _____ .

• The slope of the graph
  of $y = kx$ is ___ .

$k < 0$ $k > 0$

Example 1   *Writing a Direct Variation Equation*

The variables x and y vary directly. When $x = 7$, $y = 21$.

a. Write an equation that relates x and y.

b. Find the value of y when $x = 4$.

Solution

a. Because x and y _____, the equation is of the form
 _____. You can solve for ___ as follows.

     _____   **Write model for direct variation.**

     ___ $= k(\_\_)$ **Substitute for x and y.**

     ___ $= k$ **Divide each side by ___ .**

Answer An equation that relates x and y is _____ .

b. $y = $ ____   **Direct variation equation**

      $y = $ _____   **Substitute ___ for x.**

      $y = $ ____   **Simplify.**

Answer When $x = 4$, $y = $ ____ .

✓ *Checkpoint* **The variables x and y vary directly. Use the given values to write an equation that relates x and y. Then find the value of y when $x = -2$.**

1. $x = 6$, $y = 30$	**2.** $x = 8$, $y = 20$	**3.** $x = 3.6$, $y = 1.8$

Quick Graphs Using Slope-Intercept Form

Goals • Graph a linear equation in slope-intercept form.
• Graph and interpret equations in slope-intercept form that model real-life situations.

VOCABULARY

Slope-intercept form

_____

Parallel

SLOPE-INTERCEPT FORM OF THE EQUATION OF A LINE

The linear equation $y = mx + b$ is written in _____ form. The slope of the line is ___. The y-intercept of the line is ___ .

Example: The linear equation $y = 2x + 3$ has a slope of ___ and a y-intercept of ___ .

Example 1   *Writing Equations in Slope-Intercept Form*

Equation	Slope-Intercept Form	Slope	y-Intercept
a. $y = 5 - 2x$	$y = $ _____	$m = $ ___	$b = $ ___
b. $y = \dfrac{x-2}{3}$	$y = $ _____	$m = $ ___	$b = $ ___
c. $y = 13$	$y = $ _____	$m = $ ___	$b = $ ___
d. $2.2x - 4.4y = 0$	$y = $ _____	$m = $ ___	$b = $ ___

✔ Checkpoint Find the slope and the *y*-intercept of the graph of the equation.

1. $y = 4 - 3x$	**2.** $2x + y = -3$	**3.** $y = \dfrac{3x - 8}{4}$

Example 2   *Graphing Using Slope and y-Intercept*

Graph the equation $-2x + y = -3$.

Write the equation in slope-intercept form.

$y =$ _____

Find the slope and the *y*-intercept.

$m =$ ___ $b =$ ____

Plot the point (0, ____). Then draw a
triangle to locate a second point on the line.

$m =$ ____ $= \dfrac{\text{rise}}{\text{run}}$

Draw a line through the two points.

Example 3   *Identifying a Family of Parallel Lines*

Which of the following lines are parallel?
line *a*: $-2x + y = 4$ **line *b*:** $x + 2y = 6$ **line *c*:** $8x - 4y = 5$

Solution

Begin by writing each equation in slope-intercept form.

line *a*: $y =$ _____   **line *b*:** $y =$ _____   **line *c*:** $y =$ _____

Lines ___ and ___ are parallel because each has a slope of ___ . Line
___ is not parallel to either of the other two lines because it has

a slope of _____ .

✔ *Checkpoint* **Graph the equation.**

4. $x - y - 2 = 0$

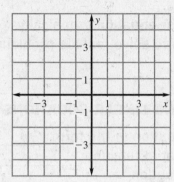

5. $2x + 3y = 9$

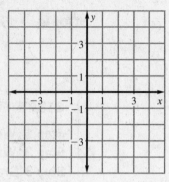

Decide whether the graphs of the two equations are parallel lines.

6. $y = 5 - 2x$, $y + 2x = 0$

7. $y = \dfrac{x - 2}{3}$, $2x + 6y = 12$

4.7 Solving Linear Equations Using Graphs

Goals • Solve a linear equation graphically.
• Use a graph to solve real-life problems.

STEPS FOR SOLVING LINEAR EQUATIONS GRAPHICALLY

Step 1 Write the equation in the form _____.
Step 2 Write the related function _____.
Step 3 Graph the equation _____.

The solution of _____ is the _____ of _____

Example 1 *Solving an Equation Graphically*

Solve $\dfrac{5}{2}x - 2 = 3x$ graphically.

> The x-intercept is __,
> so the solution is __.

1. Write the equation in the
   form $ax + b = 0$.

   $\dfrac{5}{2}x - 2 = 3x$ **Original equation**

   _____ $= 0$ **Subtract ____**
                    from each side.

2. Write the related function. $y =$ _____

3. Graph the equation $y =$ _____ .

Answer The x-intercept is ____, so the solution is $x =$ ____.

Check Check your answer algebraically.

$\dfrac{5}{2}x - 2 = 3x$ **Original equation**

$\dfrac{5}{2}(\underline{}) - 2 \stackrel{?}{=} 3(\underline{})$ **Substitute ____ for x.**

_____ $=$ ____   ____ **statement.**

> When you know two ways to solve a problem, it's a good idea to use one method to get a solution and the other method to check the solution.

Example 2 *Using a Graphing Calculator*

Use a graphing calculator to approximate the solution of the linear equation $1.25(2x - 17) = -1.25 + 6.5x$.

Solution

When you graph an equation using a graphing calculator, you do not need to simplify the equation before entering it.

_____ $= 0$ **Rewrite equation so one side is 0.**

Then use a graphing calculator (or a computer) to graph the related function

$y =$ _____ .

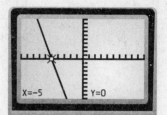

Answer The x-intercept appears to be _____, so the solution is $x =$ _____ .

✓ *Checkpoint* **Solve the equation graphically.**

1. $3x + 24 = -x$	**2.** $2x + 6 = 3x$

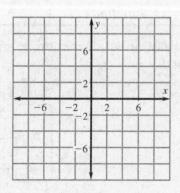 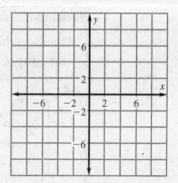

3. Use a graphing calculator to approximate the solution of the linear equation $2.65(3x - 2) = 6x + 0.55$.

4.8 Functions and Relations

Goals · Identify when a relation is a function.
· Use function notation to represent real-life situations.

VOCABULARY

Relation

Function notation

Graph of a function

Example 1 *Identifying Functions*

Decide whether the relation is a function. If so, give the domain a
the range.

a. Input   Output

```
  1 ——→ 3
  2
  3 ——→ 6
  4 ——→ 8
```

b. Input   Output

```
  1 ——→ 1
  2 ——→ 5
  3
  4 ——→ 9
```

Solution

a. The relation _____ a function because _____

_____ .

b. The relation ____ a function because _____

_____ . The domain of the function is the set o

_____ values _____ . The range is the set of _____

values _____ .

✔ **Checkpoint** Decide whether the relation is a function. If so, give the domain and the range.

1. Input   Output

```
1 ──┐
2 ──┤── 5
3 ──┤
4 ──┘
```

2. Input   Output

```
1 ──→ 2
2 ──╳── 4
3 ──┘
4 ──→ 7
```

VERTICAL LINE TEST FOR FUNCTIONS

A relation is a function of the horizontal-axis variable if and only if no _____ line passes through _____ on the graph.

You don't have use *f* to name a nction. You can se other letters, uch as *g* and *h*.

Example 2   *Evaluating a Function*

Evaluate the function for the given value of the variable.

a. $f(x) = -3x$ when $x = 2$ **b.** $g(x) = 4x + 20$ when $x = -3$

Solution

a. $f(x) = -3x$ Write original function.

         $f(\_\_\_) = -3(\_\_\_)$ Substitute ___ for *x*.

              $= \_\_\_$ Simplify.

b. $g(x) = 4x + 20$ Write original function.

         $g(\_\_\_) = 4(\_\_\_) + 20$ Substitute ___ for *x*.

              $= \_\_$ Simplify.

✔ *Checkpoint* **Evaluate the function for the given value of the variable.**

3. $f(x) = 11x + 3$ when $x = -3$	**4.** $f(x) = 6 - 1.75x$ when $x = 1$

Example 3 *Graphing a Linear Function*

Graph $f(x) = \dfrac{3}{4}x - 2$.

Rewrite the function as _____ .

_____

The *y*-intercept is ____ , so plot (0, ____).

The slope is ____ .
____

Draw a slope triangle to locate a second point on the line.

Draw a line through the two points.

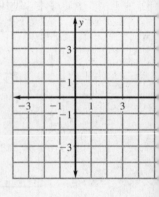

✔ *Checkpoint* **Graph the function.**

5. $f(x) = -2x + 1$	**6.** $f(x) = 4x - 3$
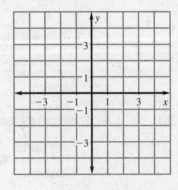	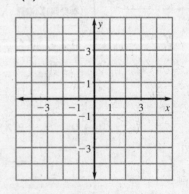

Words to Review

Give an example of the vocabulary word.

Ordered pair	*x*-coordinate, *y*-coordinate
Coordinate plane, origin, quadrants, *x*-axis, *y*-axis	Graph of an ordered pair
Scatter plot	Graph of a linear equation

Solution of an equation	x-intercept, y-intercept
Slope	Slope-intercept form
Direct variation, constant of variation	Parallel lines
Relation	Graph of a function
Function notation	

Review your notes and Chapter 4 by using the Chapter Review on pages 264–266 of your textbook.

5.1 Writing Linear Equations in Slope-Intercept Form

Goals • Use the slope-intercept form to write an equation of a line.
• Model a real-life situation with a linear function.

VOCABULARY

Slope-intercept form _____

Example 1   *Writing an Equation of a Line*

> Recall that the intercept is the coordinate of the point where the line crosses the *y*-axis.

Write an equation of the line whose slope *m* is 4 and whose *y*-intercept *b* is −3.

Solution

You are given the slope $m =$ ___ and the *y*-intercept $b =$ ____.

$y = mx + b$ Write slope-intercept form.

$y =$ __ $x +$ _____   Substitute ___ for *m* and ____ for *b*.

$y =$ __ $x -$ __   Simplify.

✔ **Checkpoint** Write an equation of the line in slope-intercept form.

1. The slope is 3; the *y*-intercept is 7.	**2.** The slope is −5; the *y*-intercept is −1.

Example 2 **Writing an Equation of a Line from a Graph**

Write an equation of the line shown in the graph.

The line intersects the y-axis at (___, ____), so the y-intercept b is ____. The line also passes through the point (____ , ___). Find the slope of the line.

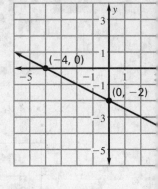

$$m = \frac{\text{rise}}{\text{run}} = \frac{\boxed{\quad - \quad}}{\boxed{\quad - \quad}} = \frac{\quad}{\quad} = \quad$$

Knowing the slope and y-intercept, you can write an equation of the line.

$y = mx + b$ Write slope-intercept form.

$y = \underline{\quad} x + \underline{\quad\quad}$ Substitute for m and b.

$y = \underline{\quad} x - \underline{\quad}$ Simplify.

✔ *Checkpoint* **Write an equation of the line shown in the graph.**

3.

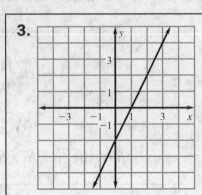

4.

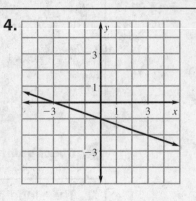

5.2 Writing Linear Equations Given the Slope and a Point

Goals • Use slope and any point on a line to write an equation of the line.
• Use a linear model to make predictions about a real-life situation.

**WRITING AN EQUATION OF A LINE
GIVEN ITS SLOPE AND A POINT**

Step 1 First find the _____. Substitute the slope m and the coordinates of the given point (x, y) into the slope-intercept form, $y = mx + b$. Then solve for the _____.

Step 2 Then write an _____. Substitute the slope m and the y-intercept b into the slope-intercept form, $y = mx + b$.

Example 1 *Writing an Equation of a Line*

Write an equation of the line that passes through the point $(-3, 5)$ and has a slope of 2.

1. Find the y-intercept. Because the line has a slope of $m = $ ___ and passes through the point $(x, y) = ($ ___ , ___ $)$, you can substitute the values $m = $ ___ , $x = $ ___ , and $y = $ ___ into the slope-intercept form and solve for b.

$$y = mx + b \qquad \text{Write slope-intercept form.}$$

$$\underline{} = (\underline{})(\underline{}) + b \qquad \text{Substitute for } m, x, \text{ and } y.$$

$$\underline{} = \underline{} + b \qquad \text{Simplify.}$$

$$\underline{} = b \qquad \text{Solve for } b.$$

The y-intercept is $b = $ ___ .

2. Write an equation of the line. Because you now know both the slope and the y-intercept, you can use the slope-intercept form.

$$y = mx + b \qquad \text{Write slope-intercept form.}$$

$$y = \underline{}x + \underline{} \qquad \text{Substitute for } m \text{ and } b.$$

Example 2   *Writing Equations of Parallel Lines*

Two nonvertical lines are parallel if and only if they have the same slope. Write an equation of the line that is parallel to the line $y = -\frac{1}{2}x - 3$ and passes through the point (2, 1).

Solution

The given line has a slope of $m = $ ___ . Because parallel lines h

the same slope, a parallel line through (2, 1) must also have a

slope of $m = $ ___ . Use this information to find the *y*-intercept.

$y = mx + b$ **Write slope-intercept form.**

$\underline{} = \left(\underline{} \right)(\underline{}) + b$ **Substitute for *m*, *x*, and *y*.**

$\underline{} = \underline{} + b$ **Simplify.**

$\underline{} = b$ **Solve for *b*.**

The *y*-intercept is $b = $ ___ .

Write an equation using the slope-intercept form.

$y = mx + b$ **Write slope-intercept form.**

$y = \underline{} x + \underline{}$ **Substitute for *m* and *b*.**

Check You can check your result graphically by graphing the original line $y = -\frac{1}{2}x - 3$ and the new line $y = \underline{} x + \underline{}$. The lines should be parallel.

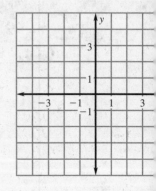

Checkpoint Write an equation of the line that passes through the point and has the given slope. Write the equation in slope-intercept form.

1. (2, 4), $m = 2$	**2.** (−3, 2), $m = −3$	**3.** (−5, −1), $m = \frac{1}{2}$

Write an equation of the line that is parallel to the given line and passes through the given point.

4. $y = 5x − 3$, (−2, 6)	**5.** $y = -\frac{3}{4}x + 2$, (3, −7)

5.3 Writing Linear Equations Given Two Points

Goals • Write an equation of a line given two points on the line.
• Use a linear equation to model a real-life problem.

WRITING AN EQUATION OF A LINE GIVEN TWO POINTS

Step 1 Find the _____. Substitute the coordinates of the two given points into the formula for slope, $m = \dfrac{y_2 - y_1}{x_2 - x_1}$.

Step 2 Find the _____. Substitute the slope m and the coordinates of one of the points into the slope-intercept form, $y = mx + b$. Then solve for the _____.

Step 3 Write an _____. Substitute the slope m and the y-intercept b into the slope-intercept form, $y = mx + b$.

Example 1   *Writing an Equation Given Two Points*

Write an equation of the line that passes through the points **(2, 8) and (−5, 1).**

Find the slope of the line. Let $(x_1, y_1) = (2, 8)$ and $(x_2, y_2) = (-5,$

$$m = \frac{y_2 - y_1}{x_2 - x_1} = \frac{}{} = \frac{}{} = \underline{}$$

Find the y-intercept. Let $m = \underline{}$, $x = 2$, and $y = 8$ and solve for

$y = mx + b$	**Write slope-intercept form.**
$\underline{} = (\underline{})(\underline{}) + b$	**Substitute for m, x, and y.**
$\underline{} = \underline{} + b$	**Simplify.**
$\underline{} = b$	**Solve for b.**

Write an equation of the line.

$y = mx + b$	**Write slope-intercept form.**
$y = \underline{}x + \underline{}$	**Substitute for m and b.**

| **Example 2** | *Writing Equations of Perpendicular Lines* |

Geometry Connection Two different nonvertical lines are perpendicular if and only if their slopes are negative reciprocals of each other.

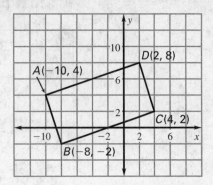

a. Show that $\overline{AB}$ and $\overline{BC}$ are perpendicular sides of *ABCD*.

b. Write equations for the lines containing $\overline{AB}$ and $\overline{BC}$.

Solution

a. Find the slopes.

For $\overline{AB}$: $m =$ _____ = ____ = ____

For $\overline{BC}$: $m =$ _____ = ____ = ____

Answer $\overline{AB}$ and $\overline{BC}$ are perpendicular because ____ is ____ _____.

b. Find the *y*-intercepts of the lines containing $\overline{AB}$ and $\overline{BC}$. Substitute the slopes from part (a) and the coordinates of one point into $y = mx + b$.

For $\overline{AB}$	For $\overline{BC}$
$y = mx + b$	$y = mx + b$
____ = (____)(____) + b	____ = $\left(\dfrac{\ }{\ }\right)$(____) + b
_____ = b	____ = b

Write an equation in slope-intercept form by substituting for *m* and *b*.

Equation of line for $\overline{AB}$

$y = mx + b$

$y =$ _____

Equation of line for $\overline{BC}$

$y = mx + b$

$y =$ _____

✔ *Checkpoint* **Write an equation in slope-intercept form of the** ▮
that passes through the points.

1. (−7, 3), (−4, 1)	**2.** (5, −6), (−2, 1)	**3.** (−2, −9), (6, −3▮

4. Write an equation of a line through (5, 4) that is perpendicular
to $y = 3x - 4$.

5.4 Fitting a Line to Data

Goals • Find a linear equation that approximates a set of data points.
• Determine whether there is a positive or negative correlation or no correlation in a set of real-life data.

VOCABULARY

Best-fitting line

Positive correlation

Negative correlation

Relatively no correlation

Example 1   *Approximating a Best-Fitting Line*

The data in the table show the height of a burning candle over time. After graphing these data points, draw a line that corresponds closely to the data. Write an equation of your line.

Time (hours)	Height (centimete
0.0	10.0
0.5	9.3
1.0	8.1
1.5	7.1
2.0	6.2
2.5	5.9
3.0	4.8
3.5	4.0
4.0	2.6

Solution

Let *x* represent the time and let *y* represent the height. To begin, plot the points given by the ordered pairs. Then sketch the line that appears to best fit the points.

Candle Height

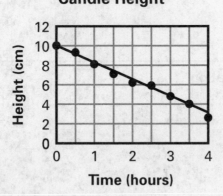

If you choose different points, you might get a different linear model. Be sure to choose points that will give you a line that is close to most of the points.

Next, find two points that lie on the line. You might choose the points (0, 10) and (3.5, 4). Find the slope of the line through thes points.

$m =$ _____   **Write slope formula.**

$=$ _____   **Substitute.**

$=$ _____   **Simplify.**

$\approx$ _____   **Decimal approximation**

Looking at the graph, the *y*-intercept is ____.

Answer An approximate equation of the best-fitting line is $y =$ _____.

Example 2 Determining Correlation

State whether x and y have a *positive correlation*, a *negative correlation*, or *relatively no correlation*.

a.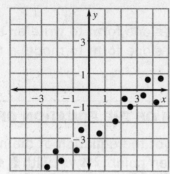

b.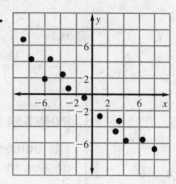

Solution

a. _____ correlation   b. _____ correlation

✓ **Checkpoint** Complete the following exercise.

1. In Example 1, suppose the best-fitting line passes through the points (1, 8.1) and (4, 2.6). Find an equation of this line.

State whether x and y have a *positive correlation*, a *negative correlation*, or *relatively no correlation*.

2.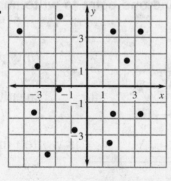

3.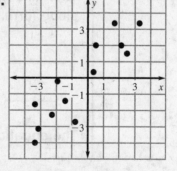

5.5 Point-Slope Form of a Linear Equation

Goals • Use the point-slope form to write an equation of a line.
• Use the point-slope form to model a real-life situation.

POINT-SLOPE FORM OF THE EQUATION OF A LINE

The point-slope form of the equation of the nonvertical line that passes through a given point (x_1, y_1) with a slope of m is

$$y - \underline{\quad} = m(x - \underline{\quad}).$$

Example 1 *Using the Point-Slope Form*

Write the point-slope form of the equation of the line that passes through (1, 1) and (5, 3).

Solution

First find the slope. Use the points $(x_1, y_1) = (1, 1)$ and $(x_2, y_2) = (5, 3)$.

$m = \underline{\qquad\qquad}$ **Use formula for slope.**

$= \underline{\qquad\quad}$ **Substitute.**

$= \underline{\quad}$ **Simplify.**

Then use the slope and one point to write an equation in point-slope form.

$\underline{\qquad\qquad} = \underline{\qquad\qquad}$ **Write point-slope form.**

$\underline{\qquad\quad} = \underline{\qquad\quad}$ **Substitute for m, x_1, and y_1.**

The equation $\underline{\qquad\qquad\qquad}$ is written in point-slope form.

Example 2   *Using the Point-Slope Form*

Write the point-slope form of the equation of the line that passes through (−6, 8) and has a slope of −1. Then rewrite the equation in slope-intercept form.

_____	= _____	Write point-slope form.
_____	= _____	Substitute for m, x_1, and y_1.
_____	= _____	Simplify.
_____	= _____	Use distributive property.
___	= _____	Add ___ to each side.

The equation _____ is written in slope-intercept form.

✔ **Checkpoint** Write the point-slope form of the equation of the line that passes through the given points.

1. (3, −4), (5, −3)	**2.** (−4, 6), (8, −3)

Write the point-slope form of the equation of the line that passes through the point and has the given slope. Then rewrite the equation in slope-intercept form.

3. (−3, −5), $m = 2$	**4.** (−1, 9), $m = -2$

5.6 The Standard Form of a Linear Equation

Goals • Write a linear equation in standard form.
• Use the standard form of an equation to model real-life situations.

VOCABULARY

Standard form

Example 1 *Writing a Linear Equation*

Write the standard form of an equation of the line passing throug (−3, 2) with a slope of −4.

Solution

You are given a point on the line and its slope, so you can write the point-slope form of the equation of the line.

_____ = _____		**Write point-slope form.**
_____ = _____		**Substitute for** m, x_1, **and** y_1.
_____ = _____		**Simplify.**
_____ = _____		**Use distributive property.**
_____ = ____		**Add ____ and __ to each side**

Answer The equation _____ is in standard form.

Example 2 *Horizontal and Vertical Lines*

Write the standard form of an equation

a. of the horizontal line.

b. of the vertical line.

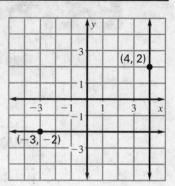

Solution

a. The horizontal line has a point with a
   y-coordinate of ____ . The standard
   form of the equation is _____ .

b. The vertical line has a point with an
   x-coordinate of ___ . The standard form
   of the equation is _____ .

✓ *Checkpoint* **Write the standard form of an equation of the line
that passes through the given point and has the given slope.**

1. (2, 5), *m* = −3	**2.** (4, −1), *m* = 0	**3.** (−4, 6), *m* = 2

**Write the standard form of an equation of the line that passes
through the two points.**

4. (3, 7), (3, 1)	**5.** (−2, −4), (5, 3)	**6.** (−1, 8), (2, −2)

Predicting with Linear Models

Goals • Determine whether a linear model is appropriate.
• Use a linear model to make a real-life prediction.

VOCABULARY

Linear interpolation

Linear extrapolation

WRITING A LINEAR MODEL

Step 1 Make a _____ of the data.

Step 2 Draw _____ the points.

Step 3 Find two points on the best-fitting line. Use these points to find the _____.

Step 4 Estimate _____ of the line.

Step 5 Use the slope and the *y*-intercept to _____ of the line.

Example 1   *Writing a Linear Model*

Internet The scatter plot at the right shows the hours per person per year that Americans use the Internet. Write a linear model for the data.

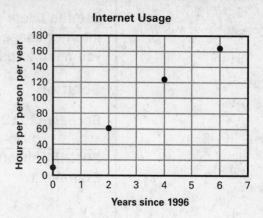

Internet Usage

Years since 1996

Solution

Draw a line that best fits the points. The line does not need to pass through any of the data points.

Find two points on the line such as (0, 10) and (6, 164). Use these points to find the slope of the line.

$$m = \underline{\hspace{2cm}} = \underline{\hspace{2.5cm}} \approx \underline{\hspace{2cm}}$$

Using a y-intercept of b = ___ and a slope of m = ___, you can write an equation of the line.

$y = \underline{\hspace{2.5cm}}$ **Write slope-intercept form.**

$y = \underline{\hspace{2.5cm}}$ **Substitute for m and b.**

Answer A linear model for the hours per person per year that Americans use the Internet is $y = \underline{\hspace{2.5cm}}$.

✔ *Checkpoint* **Complete the following exercise.**

1. In Example 1, suppose the line passes through the points (0, 10) and (3, 97). Write a linear model for the data.

Example 2 *Linear Interpolation and Linear Extrapolation*

Use the linear model you found in Example 1 to estimate the Internet usage (in hours per person per year) in 2012. Tell whethe you need to use *linear interpolation* or *linear extrapolation*.

Solution

Because 2012 is to the right of all of the given data, you will use _____ . You can estimate the Internet usage in 2012 by substituting $x =$ ___ into the linear model from Example 1.

$y =$ _____   **Write linear model.**

$=$ _____   **Substitute for x.**

$=$ _____   **Simplify.**

Answer The model estimates that the Internet usage in 2012 will about _____ hours per person per year.

✓ *Checkpoint* Use the linear model you found in Example 1 to estimate the Internet usage (in hours per person per year) in the given year. Tell whether you need to use *linear interpolation* or *linear extrapolation*.

2. 2014	3. 1997

Words to Review

Give an example of the vocabulary word.

Slope-intercept form	Best-fitting line
Positive correlation	Negative correlation
Point-slope form	Standard form
Linear interpolation	Linear extrapolation

Review your notes and Chapter 5 by using the Chapter Review on pages 324–326 of your textbook.

6.1 Solving One-Step Linear Inequalities

Goals • Graph linear inequalities in one variable.
         • Solve one-step linear inequalities.

VOCABULARY

Graph of a linear inequality in one variable

Equivalent inequalities

Example 1   *Write and Graph a Linear Inequality*

Speed Limit You are traveling in a section of town where the s[peed] limit is 35 miles per hour. Write an inequality to describe the sp[eeds] that are over the speed limit in that section. Graph the inequalit[y.]

Solution

Speds _____ 35 miles per hour are against the law. L[et]
represent _____.

_____   **Write linear inequality.**

> Remember that an open dot is used for < or > and a solid dot is used for ≤ or ≥.

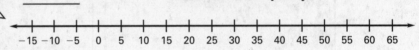

✔ *Checkpoint* **Complete the following exercise.**

---

1. You must be 18 years old or older to vote in the town election[.] Write an inequality to describe the ages of people allowed to vote in the town election. Graph the inequality.

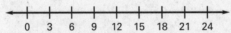

TRANSFORMATIONS THAT PRODUCE EQUIVALENT INEQUALITIES

Transformation	Original Inequality		Equivalent Inequality
• Add the same number to each side.	$x - 3 < 5$	Add ___.	_____
• Subtract the same number from each side.	$x + 6 \geq 9$	Subtract ___.	_____
• Multiply each side by the same _____ number.	$\frac{1}{2}x > 3$	Multiply by ___.	_____
• Divide each side by the same _____ number.	$3x \leq 9$	Divide by ___.	_____
• Multiply each side by the same _____ number and _____ the inequality symbol.	$-x < 4$	Multiply by _____.	_____
• Divide each side by the same _____ number and _____ the inequality symbol.	$-2x \leq 6$	Divide by _____.	_____

Example 2   Solving an Inequality

Solve $x + 11 \leq 7$. Graph the solution.

$x + 11 \leq 7$ Write original inequality.

$x + 11 - \underline{\ \ } \leq 7 - \underline{\ \ }$ Subtract ___ from each side.

___ ___ ___   Simplify.

Answer The solution is all real numbers _____.
Check several numbers in the original inequality.

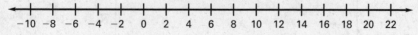

> Check several possible solutions by substituting them in the original inequality. Also try some numbers that are *not* solutions to make sure that they do not satisfy the original inequality.

Example 3   Solving an Inequality

$$\frac{b}{5} \geq 12$$ **Original inequality**

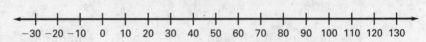___ · $\frac{b}{5}$ ___ ___ · 12   **Multiply each side by ___ .**

_____   **Simplify.**

Answer The solution is all real numbers _____
_____ . Check several numbers in the original inequality.

$$\begin{array}{c} \xleftarrow{\quad} \!\!\!\! \vert\ \vert\ \vert\ \vert\ \vert\ \vert\ \vert\ \vert\ \vert\ \vert\ \vert\ \vert\ \vert\ \vert\ \vert\ \vert\ \vert \!\!\!\! \xrightarrow{\quad} \\ {\scriptstyle -30\ -20\ -10\ \ \ 0\ \ \ 10\ \ 20\ \ 30\ \ 40\ \ 50\ \ 60\ \ 70\ \ 80\ \ 90\ \ 100\ 110\ 120\ 130} \end{array}$$

Example 4   Solving an Inequality

$$-1.8n < -4.5$$ **Original inequality**

$$\frac{-1.8n}{\boxed{}} \ \_\!\_ \ \frac{-4.5}{\boxed{}}$$ **Divide each side by _____ and
_____ inequality symbol.**

_____   **Simplify.**

Answer The solution is all real numbers _____ . Check
several numbers in the original inequality.

$$\begin{array}{c} \xleftarrow{\quad} \!\!\!\! \vert\ \vert\ \vert\ \vert\ \vert\ \vert\ \vert\ \vert\ \vert\ \vert\ \vert\ \vert\ \vert\ \vert\ \vert\ \vert\ \vert \!\!\!\! \xrightarrow{\quad} \\ {\scriptstyle 1.7\ \ 1.8\ \ 1.9\ \ 2.0\ \ 2.1\ \ 2.2\ \ 2.3\ \ 2.4\ \ 2.5\ \ 2.6\ \ 2.7\ \ 2.8\ \ 2.9\ \ 3.0\ \ 3.1\ \ 3.2\ \ 3.3} \end{array}$$

✔ **Checkpoint** Solve the inequality. Graph the solution.

2. $x - 4 > -13$	**3.** $-10y \geq 50$
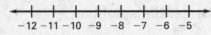	

$$\begin{array}{c} \xleftarrow{\quad} \!\!\!\! \vert\ \vert\ \vert\ \vert\ \vert\ \vert\ \vert\ \vert \!\!\!\! \xrightarrow{\quad} \\ {\scriptstyle -12\ -11\ -10\ \ -9\ \ -8\ \ -7\ \ -6\ \ -5} \end{array}$$

$$\begin{array}{c} \xleftarrow{\quad} \!\!\!\! \vert\ \vert\ \vert\ \vert\ \vert\ \vert\ \vert\ \vert \!\!\!\! \xrightarrow{\quad} \\ {\scriptstyle -8\ \ -7\ \ -6\ \ -5\ \ -4\ \ -3\ \ -2\ \ -1} \end{array}$$

6.2 Solving Multi-Step Linear Inequalities

Goals • Solve multi-step linear inequalities.
• Use linear inequalities to model and solve real-life problems.

Example 1 *Using More than One Step*

Solve $\frac{5}{6}x - 2 \leq 18$.

Solution

$\frac{5}{6}x - 2 \leq 18$ Write original inequality.

$\frac{5}{6}x \leq$ _____   Add ___ to each side.

x ___ ___   Multiply each side by ___ .

Answer The solution is all real numbers _____ .

Example 2 *Multiplying or Dividing by a Negative Number*

Solve $9 - 3t < 7 + 2t$.

Solution

$9 - 3t < 7 + 2t$ Write original inequality.

$-3t <$ ___ $+ 2t$ Subtract ___ from each side.

_____ $<$ _____   Subtract ____ from each side.

_____   Divide each side by ____ . _____
                 inequality symbol.

Answer The solution is all real numbers _____ .

Example 3   *Writing and Using a Linear Model*

Long Distance Calls You pay $.045 per minute for long distance calls, and a monthly fee of $5. How many minutes of long distance can you use to keep within your monthly long distance budget of $20?

Solution

The amount spent on calls plus the monthly fee must be _____ _____ your monthly budget.

Verbal Model	Cost per minute	×	Number of minutes	+	Monthly fee	≤	Monthly budget

Labels   Cost per minute = _____   (dollars per minute)

Number of minutes = m (minutes)

Monthly fee = ___   (dollars)

Monthly budget = ___   (dollars)

Algebraic Model

_____   Write algebraic model.

_____   Subtract ___ from each side.

_____   Divide each side by _____ .

Answer You can use _____ of long distance per month to keep within your monthly long distance budget.

Check You can check your result graphically by graphing equations for the total cost and the budget separately.

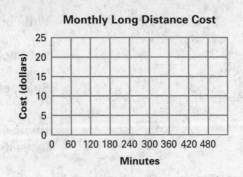

Monthly Long Distance Cost

✓ *Checkpoint* **Solve the inequality.**

1. $17 - x \geq 12$	2. $3x + 2 > x - 8$

3. Your school carnival charges $2 for admission and $.50 for each game. You go to the carnival with $5.50. Write and solve an inequality that represents the possible number of games you can play. What is the maximum number of games you can play?

6.3 Solving Compound Inequalities

Goals • Write, solve, and graph compound inequalities.
• Model a real-life situation with a compound inequality.

VOCABULARY

Compound inequality

Example 1   *Writing Compound Inequalities*

Write an inequality that represents the set of numbers and graph the inequality.

a. All real numbers that are greater than or equal to −5 *and* less than −2.

b. All real numbers that are greater than or equal to 3 *or* less than −3.

c. All real numbers that are greater than or equal to −4 *and* less than or equal to 0.

Solution

a.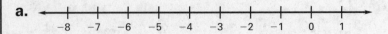

$$-5 \underline{\quad} x \underline{\quad} -2$$

b.

$$x \underline{\quad} 3 \ or \ x \underline{\quad} -3$$

c.

$$-4 \underline{\quad} x \underline{\quad} 0$$

Example 2   *Solving a Compound Inequality with And*

Solve $-27 < 5x - 7 < 18$. Graph the solution.

Solution

Isolate the variable x between the two inequality symbols.

$-27 < 5x - 7 < 18$ **Write original inequality.**

_____   **Add ___ to each expression.**

_____   **Divide each expression by ___ .**

Answer The solution is all real numbers that are _____

_____ .

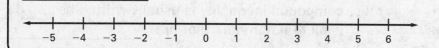

Example 3   *Solving a Compound Inequality with Or*

Solve $3x + 1 \le -2$ or $7x - 3 \ge 18$. Graph the solution.

Solution

A solution of this inequality is a solution of either of its simple parts. You can solve each part separately.

$3x + 1 \le -2$ *or* $7x - 3 \ge 18$

_____   *or*   _____

_____   *or*   _____

Answer The solution is all real numbers that are _____

_____ .

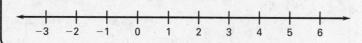

Example 4   *Reversing Both Inequality Symbols*

Solve $-7 < -2x + 1 \le -3$. Graph the solution.

Solution

Isolate the variable x between the two inequality symbols.

$-7 < -2x + 1 \le -3$ Write original inequality.

_____   Subtract ___ from each expression.

_____   Divide each expression by _____ and

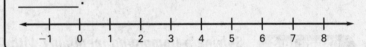

Answer To match the order of numbers on a number line, this compound inequality is usually written as _____. The solution is all real numbers that are _____

_____.

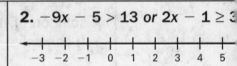

✔ *Checkpoint* **Solve the compound inequality. Graph the solution.**

1. $-25 \le 11x - 3 < 8$	**2.** $-9x - 5 > 13$ *or* $2x - 1 \ge 3$

Example 5   *Modeling with a Compound Inequality*

Playing Tag You are playing tag with your friends. You are 20 feet from base and the person who is "It" is 30 feet from base. Let d represent the distance between you and the person who is "It."

a. What is the smallest possible value of d?

b. What is the largest possible value of d?

c. Write an inequality that describes all the possible values of d.

Solution

Draw a Diagram A good way to begin this problem is to draw a diagram with the base at the center of a circle.

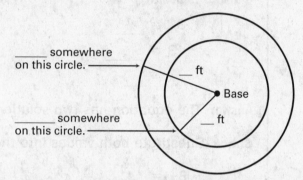

_____ somewhere on this circle.

__ ft

Base

_____ somewhere on this circle.

__ ft

You are somewhere on the circle with radius ____ feet and center at base. The person who is "It" is somewhere on the circle with radius ____ feet and center at base.

a. If you both are on the same line on the same side of base, the distance is ____ feet.

b. If you both are on the same line but on opposite sides of base, the distance is ____ feet.

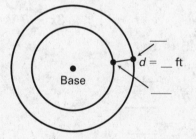

$d = $ __ ft

Base

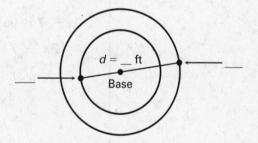

$d = $ __ ft

Base

c. The values of d can be described by the inequality

_____ .

6.4 Solving Absolute-Value Equations and Inequalities

Goals • Solve absolute-value equations and inequalities.

Example 1 *Solving an Absolute-Value Equation*

Solve $|x + 3| = 11$.

Because $|x + 3| = 11$, the expression $x + 3$ can be equal to
____ or ____ .

$x + 3$ is positive	$x + 3$ is negative
$|x + 3| =$ ____	$|x + 3| =$ ____
$x + 3 =$ ____	$x + 3 =$ ____
$x =$ ____	$x =$ ____

Answer The equation has two solutions: ____ and ____ .

Check Substitute both values into the original equation.

$|__ + 3| = $ ____ $=$ ____ $|____ + 3| = $ ____ $=$ ____

Example 2 *Solving an Absolute-Value Equation*

Solve $|3x - 7| + 5 = 9$.

Isolate the absolute-value expression on one side of the equation.

$3x - 7$ is positive	$3x - 7$ is negative
$|3x - 7| + 5 = 9$	$|3x - 7| + 5 = 9$
$|3x - 7| =$ ____	$|3x - 7| =$ ____
$3x - 7 =$ ____	$3x - 7 =$ ____
$3x =$ ____	$3x =$ ____
$x =$ ____ $=$ ____	$x =$ ____

Answer The equation has two solutions: ____ and ____ . Check these
solutions in the original equation.

SOLVING ABSOLUTE-VALUE EQUATIONS AND INEQUALITIES

Each absolute-value equation or inequality is rewritten as two equations or two inequalities joined by *and* or *or*.

Notice that when an absolute value is *less than* a number, the inequalities are connected by *and*. When an absolute value is *greater than* a number, the inequalities are connected by *or*.

- $|ax + b| < c$ **means** $ax + b \_\_\_ c$ and $ax + b \_\_\_ -c$.
- $|ax + b| \le c$ **means** $ax + b \_\_\_ c$ and $ax + b \_\_\_ -c$.
- $|ax + b| = c$ **means** $ax + b \_\_\_ c$ or $ax + b \_\_\_ -c$.
- $|ax + b| > c$ **means** $ax + b \_\_\_ c$ or $ax + b \_\_\_ -c$.
- $|ax + b| \ge c$ **means** $ax + b \_\_\_ c$ or $ax + b \_\_\_ -c$.

Example 3 *Solving an Absolute-Value Inequality*

Solve $|5x - 7| \le 23$.

Solution

$5x - 7$ is positive	$5x - 7$ is negative
$\|5x - 7\| \le 23$	$\|5x - 7\| \le 23$
$5x - 7 \le \_\_\_\_\_$	$5x - 7 \ge \_\_\_\_\_$ ← **Reverse inequality symbol.**
$5x \le \_\_\_$	$5x \ge \_\_\_\_\_$
$x \le \_\_\_$	$x \ge \dfrac{_____}{_____} = $

Answer The solution is all real numbers $_____$

$_____$, which can be written as

$_____$.

Example 4 *Solving an Absolute-Value Inequality*

Solve $|x - 11| + 2 > 8$.

Solution

$x - 11$ is positive	$x - 11$ is negative	
$|x - 11| + 2 > 8$	$|x - 11| + 2 > 8$	
$|x - 11| > \underline{\hspace{1cm}}$	$|x - 11| > \underline{\hspace{1cm}}$	
$x - 11 > \underline{\hspace{1cm}}$	$x - 11 < \underline{\hspace{1cm}}$	← **Reverse**
$x > \underline{\hspace{1cm}}$	$x < \underline{\hspace{1cm}}$	**inequality symbol.**

Answer The solution is all real numbers _____
_____ , which can be written as the compound inequality
_____ .

✔ *Checkpoint* **Solve the equation.**

1. $|x - 3| = 7$	**2.** $|4x + 10| = 34$

Solve the inequality.

3. $|3x| \geq 18$	**4.** $|x - 7| < 16$

Graphing Linear Inequalities in Two Variables

Goals • Graph a linear inequality in two variables.
• Model a real-life situation using a linear inequality in two variables.

VOCABULARY

Linear inequality

Solution of a linear inequality

Graph of a linear inequality

Half-plane

Example 1   *Checking Solutions of a Linear Inequality*

Check whether the ordered pair is a solution of $8x - 4y \geq 3$.

a. (0, 0)   **b.** (1, −1)

Solution

(x, y)	$8x - 4y \geq 3$	Conclusion
a. (0, 0)	8(___) − 4(___) = ___ ___ 3	(0, 0) _____ a solution.
b. (1, −1)	8(___) − 4(___) = ___ ___ 3	(1, −1) _____ a solution.

GRAPHING A LINEAR INEQUALITY

Step 1 Graph the corresponding equation. Use a _____ line for inequalities with > or < to show that the points on the line are not solutions. Use a _____ line for inequalities with ≥ or ≤ to show that the points on the line are solutions.

Step 2 The line drawn in Step 1 separates the coordinate plane into two _____ . Test a point in one of the half-planes to find whether it is a solution of the inequality.

Step 3 If the test point is a solution, _____ the half-plane it is in. If not, _____ the other half-plane.

Example 2 *Graphing a Linear Inequality*

Sketch the graph of x > 3.

> You can test any point that is not on the line. The origin is often used because it is easy to evaluate expressions in which 0 is substituted for each variable.

1. Graph the corresponding equation
   x = 3, a _____ line. Use a _____
   line.

2. Test a point. The origin (0, 0) _____
   a solution and it lies to the _____
   of the line. So, the graph of x > 3 is all
   points to the _____ of the line x = 3.

3. _____ the region to the _____
   of the line.

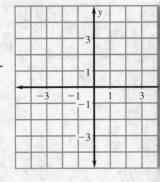

✔ *Checkpoint* **Sketch the graph of the inequality.**

1. y ≤ −4

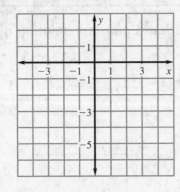

2. x < 2

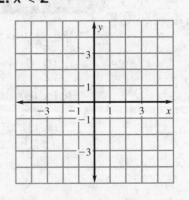

Example 3 *Writing in Slope-Intercept Form*

Sketch the graph of $2x + 3y < 6$.

Solution

The corresponding equation is _____ . To graph this line, you can first write the equation in _____ form.

$$3y = \underline{} + 6$$

$$y = -\frac{2}{3}x + \underline{}$$

Then graph the line that has a slope

of $-\frac{2}{3}x$ and a y-intercept of ___ . Use a

_____ line. The origin $(0, 0)$ ___ a solution and it lies _____ the line. So, the graph of $2x + 3y < 6$ is all points

_____ the line $y = -\frac{2}{3}x + \underline{}$.

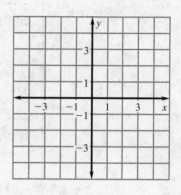

✓ *Checkpoint* **Sketch the graph of the inequality.**

3. $x + y \geq -2$	**4.** $5x - y < 3$
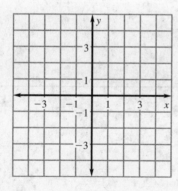	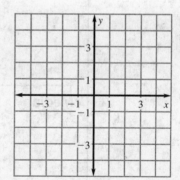

Stem-and-Leaf Plots and Mean, Median, and Mode

Goals • Make and use a stem-and-leaf plot to put data in order.
• Find the mean, median, and mode of data.

VOCABULARY

Stem-and-leaf plot

Measure of central tendency

Mean

Median

Mode

Example 1   *Making a Stem-and-Leaf Plot*

Figure Skating In a skating competition, a figure skater's technical marks were 4.0, 5.5, 5.8, 4.3, 3.9, 0.0, 5.0, 4.1, 3.5, and 4.1. Make a stem-and-leaf plot to display the data.

Solution

Use the digits in the ones' place for the _____ and the digits in the tenths' place for the _____ . The _____ shows you how to interpret the digits.

Unordered stem-and-leaf plot		Ordered stem-and-leaf plot

Stems 0
1
2   Leaves
3
4
5

0
1
2
3
4
5

Key: 4 | 3 = ____   Key: 4 | 3 = ____

Example 2   *Finding the Mean, Median, and Mode*

Find the mean, median, and mode(s) of the figure skater's technical marks given in Example 1.

1. To find the mean, add the 10 marks and divide by ___ .

   mean =

+	+	+	+	+	+	+	+	+

   = _____ ≈ _____

2. To find the median, write the marks in _____ and find the _____ of the two _____ numbers. To order the marks, use the ordered stem-and-leaf plot in Example 1.

   _____

   The two middle numbers are ____ and ____ .
   The median is the average of these two numbers: ____ .

3. To find the mode(s), use the ordered list in step 2. The mode is ____ .

Example 3   *A Bell-Shaped Distribution*

Essay questions on a history test are given a score from 0 to 10. Find the median and mode of the data given in the histogram.

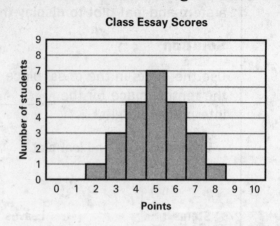

Class Essay Scores

Solution The tallest bar is at ___ points, so that is the mode. The number of responses to the left of that bar is the same as the number of responses to the right, so ___ points is the _____.

✓ *Checkpoint* Make an ordered stem-and-leaf plot of the data. Then find the mean, median, and mode(s).

1. 15, 10, 17, 23, 19, 15, 22, 16, 45, 20, 13, 12, 17, 15

2. 89, 72, 79, 60, 51, 54, 60, 89, 67, 60, 58, 56, 77, 55, 78

Box-and-Whisker Plots

Goals • Draw a box-and-whisker plot to organize real-life data.
 • Read and interpret a box-and-whisker plot of real-life data.

VOCABULARY

Box-and-whisker plot
_____

Second quartile
_____

_____

First quartile
_____

Third quartile
_____

Example 1   *Finding Quartiles*

Find the first, second, and third quartiles of the data.

 $15, 8, -5, 0, 2, 11, 10, -5, 4, 4, -3, 10, 7, 2, -2, 1$

Solution

Begin by writing the numbers in increasing order. You must find the
second quartile before you find the first and third quartiles.

_____

Second quartile: $\dfrac{2 + 4}{2} =$ ___

First quartile: $\dfrac{-2 + 0}{2} =$ ___

Third quartile: $\dfrac{8 + 10}{2} =$ ___

DRAWING A BOX-AND-WHISKER PLOT

Step 1 Plot the least number, the first quartile, the second quartile, the third quartile, and the greatest number on a number line.

Step 2 Draw a line from _____ to _____ below your number line. Plot the same points o that line.

Step 3 Make a box from _____ to _____ Draw a vertical line in the box at _____. The "whiskers" connect the box to the least and greatest numbers.

Example 2 *Drawing a Box-and-Whisker Plot*

Draw a box-and-whisker plot of the data in Example 1.

1. Plot the least number, _____, the first quartile, _____, the second quartile, ___, third quartile, ___, and the greatest number, _____, on a number line.

2. Draw a line from _____ to ___ below the number line. Plot the points _____, _____, ___, ___, and _____ on that line.

3. Make a box from _____ to ___. Draw a vertical line in the box at ___.

```
 ┼──┼──┼──┼──┼──┼──┼──┼──┼──┼──┼──┼──┼──┼──┼
-10 -8  -6  -4  -2   0   2   4   6   8  10  12  14  16  18
```

✔ *Checkpoint* **Complete the following exercise.**

1. Make a box-and-whisker plot of the data.
   3, 6, 1, 4, 5, 4, 4, 7, 3, 3, 3, 1, 2, 3, 4, 4, 6, 5, 3, 3, 1, 2, 5, 4, 4, 5, 4, 2, 4, 5

Example 3 | *Interpreting a Box-and-Whisker Plot*

Gas Mileage The box-and-whisker plots below show the city-driving gas mileages for selected midsize cars and standard size 2WD pickup trucks.

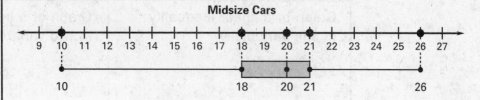

Midsize Cars

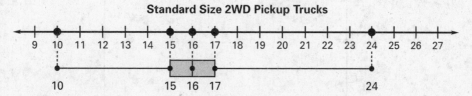

Standard Size 2WD Pickup Trucks

a. What is the median city-driving gas mileage for the midsize cars? for the pickup trucks?

b. Which vehicle has the overall better city-driving gas mileage?

c. How else do the data sets differ?

Solution

a. The median city-driving gas mileage for the midsize cars is ____ miles per gallon. The median city-driving gas mileage for the pickup trucks is ____ miles per gallon.

b. The _____ get better city-driving gas mileage than the _____. Three-fourths of the midsize cars have a gas mileage of ____ miles per gallon or higher, whereas only one-fourth of the pickup trucks have a gas mileage of ____ miles per gallon or higher.

c. There is a little more variability in the gas mileages for the _____ than for the _____.

The gas mileages for the midsize cars span from ____ to ____ miles per gallon, while the gas mileages for the pickup trucks span from ____ to ____ miles per gallon.

The difference in the extremes of gas mileages for the midsize cars is ____ miles per gallon, while the difference in the extremes of gas mileages for the pickup trucks is ____ miles per gallon.

Words to Review

Give an example of the vocabulary word.

Graph of a linear inequality in one variable	Graph of a linear inequality in two variables
Equivalent Inequalities	Compound inequality
Linear inequality in x and y	Solution of a linear inequality

Stem-and-leaf plot	Mean, Median, Mode

Box-and-whisker plot

Review your notes and Chapter 6 by using the Chapter Review on pages 384–386 of your textbook.

7.1 Solving Linear Systems by Graphing

Goals • Solve a system of linear equations by graphing.
• Model a real-life problem using a linear system.

VOCABULARY

System of linear equations

Solution of a system of linear equations

SOLVING A LINEAR SYSTEM USING GRAPH-AND-CHECK

To use the graph-and-check method to solve a system of linear equations in two variables, use the following steps.

Step 1 Write each equation in a form that is _____.

Step 2 Graph both equations in the _____.

Step 3 Estimate the coordinates of the _____.

Step 4 Check the coordinates algebraically by _____ into each equation of the _____ linear system.

Example 1   *Using the Graph-and-Check Method*

Solve the linear system graphically. Check the solution algebraically.

$5x + 4y = -12$ **Equation 1**

$3x - 4y = -20$ **Equation 2**

Solution

1. Write each equation in a form that is easy to graph, such as slope-intercept form.

Equation 1	**Equation 2**
$5x + 4y = -12$	$3x - 4y = -20$
$4y = \underline{\hspace{2cm}}$	$-4y = \underline{\hspace{2cm}}$
$y = \underline{\hspace{1.5cm}}$	$y = \underline{\hspace{1.5cm}}$
slope: $\underline{\hspace{1cm}}$	slope: $\underline{\hspace{1cm}}$
y-intercept: $\underline{\hspace{1cm}}$	y-intercept: $\underline{\hspace{1cm}}$

2. Graph these equations.

3. The two lines appear to intersect at (___ , ___).

4. To check (___ , ___) as a solution algebraically, substitute ___ for x and ___ for y in each original equation.

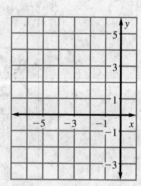

Equation 1	**Equation 2**
$5x + 4y = -12$	$3x - 4y = -20$
$5(\underline{\hspace{1cm}}) + 4(\underline{\hspace{0.7cm}}) \stackrel{?}{=} -12$	$3(\underline{\hspace{1cm}}) - 4(\underline{\hspace{0.7cm}}) \stackrel{?}{=} -20$
$\underline{\hspace{1.5cm}} + \underline{\hspace{0.7cm}} \stackrel{?}{=} -12$	$\underline{\hspace{1.5cm}} - \underline{\hspace{0.7cm}} \stackrel{?}{=} -20$
$\underline{\hspace{1.5cm}} \underline{\hspace{0.5cm}} -12$	$\underline{\hspace{1.5cm}} \underline{\hspace{0.5cm}} -20$

Answer Because (___ , ___) is a solution of each equation in the linear system, (___ , ___) is a solution of the linear system.

1. $3x - 4y = 4$

$x + 2y = 8$

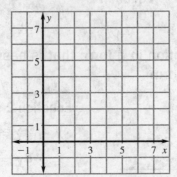

2. $5x + 2y = 4$

$9x + 2y = 12$

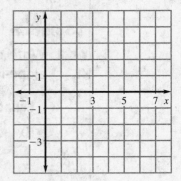

3. $y = -2x - 3$

$2x + 5y = 25$

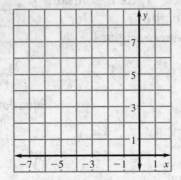

4. $y = 3x + 4$

$7x - 3y = -6$

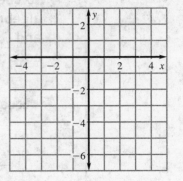

7.2 Solving Linear Systems by Substitution

Goals • Use substitution to solve a linear system.
• Model a real-life situation using a linear system.

SOLVING A LINEAR SYSTEM BY SUBSTITUTION

Step 1 Solve one of the equations for one of its _____ .

Step 2 Substitute the expression from Step 1 into the other equation and solve for the _____ .

Step 3 Substitute the value from _____ into the revised equation from _____ and solve.

Step 4 Check the solution in each of the _____ equations.

Example 1   *Choosing an Equation to Solve*

Tell which equation you would use to isolate a variable. Explain your reasoning.

a. $6x + y = -5$ **Equation 1**   b. $5c - 2d = 1$ **Equation 1**
   $2x - 3y = 10$ **Equation 2** $c + 3d = 0$ **Equation 2**

Solution

a. It would be easiest to isolate ___ in Equation ___ because the variable has _____ .

b. It would be easiest to isolate ___ in Equation ___ because the variable has _____ .

Example 2 *The Substitution Method*

Solve the linear system.

$$2x - 5y = -13 \qquad \text{Equation 1}$$
$$x + 3y = -1 \qquad \text{Equation 2}$$

Solution

1. Solve for x in Equation 2 because it is easy to isolate x.

$$x = \underline{\hspace{2cm}} \qquad \text{Revised Equation 2}$$

2. Substitute \underline{\hspace{1.5cm}} for x in Equation 1 and solve for y.

$$2x - 5y = -13 \qquad \text{Write Equation 1.}$$
$$2(\underline{\hspace{1.5cm}}) - 5y = -13 \qquad \text{Substitute for } x.$$
$$\underline{\hspace{1.5cm}} - 5y = -13 \qquad \text{Distribute.}$$
$$\underline{\hspace{1.5cm}} = -13 \qquad \text{Simplify.}$$
$$\underline{\hspace{1.5cm}} = \underline{\hspace{1cm}} \qquad \text{Add \_\_ to each side.}$$
$$y = \underline{\hspace{0.5cm}} \qquad \text{Solve for } y.$$

3. To find the value of x, substitute __ for y in the revised Equation 2 and solve for x.

$$x = \underline{\hspace{2cm}} \qquad \text{Write revised Equation 2.}$$
$$x = \underline{\hspace{2cm}} \qquad \text{Substitute for } y.$$
$$x = \underline{\hspace{1cm}} \qquad \text{Simplify.}$$

4. Check that (\underline{\hspace{1cm}} , __) is a solution by substituting \underline{\hspace{1cm}} for x and __ for y in each of the original equations.

Equation 1	Equation 2
$2x - 5y = -13$	$x + 3y = -1$
$2(\underline{\hspace{0.8cm}}) - 5(\underline{\hspace{0.4cm}}) \stackrel{?}{=} -13$	$\underline{\hspace{0.8cm}} + 3(\underline{\hspace{0.4cm}}) \stackrel{?}{=} -1$
$\underline{\hspace{0.8cm}} - \underline{\hspace{0.4cm}} \stackrel{?}{=} -13$	$\underline{\hspace{0.8cm}} + \underline{\hspace{0.4cm}} \stackrel{?}{=} -1$
$\underline{\hspace{1cm}} \underline{\hspace{0.5cm}} -13$	$\underline{\hspace{1cm}} \underline{\hspace{0.5cm}} -1$

Answer The solution is (\underline{\hspace{1cm}} , __).

Checkpoint Tell which equation you would use to isolate a variable. Explain your reasoning.

1. $x - 2y = 0$ $x - 8y = -5$	**2.** $4x + 2y = 10$ $7x - y = 12$

Use the substitution method to solve the linear system.

3. $y = x - 1$ $x - 5y = -15$	**4.** $y = -5x + 3$ $3x + 2y = -8$

7.3 Solving Linear Systems by Linear Combinations

Goals • Use linear combinations to solve a system of linear equatio
• Model a real-life problem using a system of linear equatio

VOCABULARY

Linear combination

Example 1 *Using Addition*

Solve the linear system. $7x + 2y = -6$ **Equation 1**
                              $5x - 2y = 6$ **Equation 2**

Solution

The equations are already arranged with like terms in columns.

The coefficients for y are already opposites.

Add the equations to get an equation in one variable.

$7x + 2y = -6$	Write Equation 1.
$\underline{5x - 2y = 6}$	Write Equation 2.
$\underline{} = \underline{}$	Add equations.
$\underline{} = \underline{}$	Solve for ___.

Substitute ___ for ___ in the first equation and solve for ___ .

| $7(\underline{}) + 2y = -6$ | Substitute for ___ . |
| $\underline{} = \underline{}$ | Solve for ___ . |

Check that (___ , ____) is a solution by substituting ___ for *x* and ____ for *y* in each of the original equations.

Answer The solution is (___ , ____).

Example 2 *Using Multiplication First*

Solve the linear system: $3x - 5y = 15$ **Equation 1**

                                 $2x + 4y = -1$ **Equation 2**

Solution

The equations are already arranged. You can get the coefficients of x to be opposites by multiplying the first equation by ___ and the second equation by ____ .

$3x - 5y = 15$ **Multiply by __ .**   ⟶   ___ $x -$ ___ $y =$ ___

$2x + 4y = -1$ **Multiply by ____ .**   ⟶   ____ $x -$ ___ $y =$ __

Add the equations and solve for ___ .   _____ $=$ __

                                               __ $=$ _____

Substitute _____ for __ in the second equation and solve for __ .

        $2x + 4y = -1$ **Write Equation 2.**

    $2x + 4($ _____ $) = -1$ **Substitute for __ .**

        $2x -$ __ $= -1$ **Simplify.**

            __ $=$ ___   **Solve for __ .**

Answer The solution is (_____ , _____).

✔ *Checkpoint* Use linear combinations to solve the system of linear equations.

1. $4x + y = -4$
     $-4x + 2y = 16$
	2. $7x + y = 2$
	     $5x + 2y = 4$

Example 3 *Arranging Like Terms in Columns*

Solve the linear system.　　$3y = -6 - 4x$　　**Equation 1**

　　　　　　　　　　　　　　$7x + 3y = -15$　　**Equation 2**

Solution

First arrange the equations.

$$4x + 3y = -6$$ 　　**Rearrange Equation 1.**
$$7x + 3y = -15$$ 　　**Write Equation 2.**

You can get the coefficients of y to be opposites by multiplying the second equation by ____ .

$4x + 3y = \;\;\; -6$ 　　　　　　　　　　　　　　　$4x + \;\;\; 3y = -6$

$7x + 3y = -15$　**Multiply by ___ .** ➤　____ $x -$ __$y =$ ____

Add the equations and solve for __ .　　　　____　　　$=$ __

　　　　　　　　　　　　　　　　　　　　　　　　　　__ $=$ __

Substitute ____ for __ in the second equation and solve for __ .

$$7x + 3y = -15$$ 　　　　**Write Equation 2.**

$$7(\underline{\quad}) + 3y = -15$$ 　　**Substitute for __ .**

$$\underline{\quad} + 3y = -15$$ 　　**Simplify.**

$$\underline{\quad} = \underline{\quad}$$ 　　　　　**Solve for __ .**

Answer The solution is (____ , __).

✔ *Checkpoint* **Use linear combinations to solve the system of linear equations.**

3. $x - 3y - 8 = 0$ 　　$4y = 11 - 3x$	**4.** $6x - 23 = -5y$ 　　$9x + 32 = 2y$

7.4 Applications of Linear Systems

Goals • Choose the best method to solve a system of linear equations.
• Use a system to model real-life problems.

Example 1 *Choosing a Solution Method*

Health Food A health food store mixes granola and raisins to make 20 pounds of raisin granola. Granola costs them $4 per pound and raisins cost them $5 per pound. How many pounds of each should they include if they want the mixture to cost them a total of $85? Write a verbal and algebraic model for the problem.

Solution

Verbal Model

Pounds of granola	+		=	Total Pounds

Price of granola	·		+	Price of raisins	·

	=	Total cost

Labels
Pounds of granola = ___	(pounds)
Pounds of raisins = ___	(pounds)
Total pounds = ___	(pounds)
Price of granola = ___	(dollars per pound)
Price of raisins = ___	(dollars per pound)
Total cost = ___	(dollars)

Algebraic Model
___ + ___ = ___   Equation 1
___ + ___ = ___   Equation 2

Example 2   *Solving a Mixture Problem*

Solve the linear system in Example 1 and answer the question.

Solution

The algebraic model is as follows.

___ + ___ = ___   **Equation 1**

___ + ___ = ___   **Equation 2**

Because the coefficients of x and y are 1 in Equation 1, _____ is most convenient. Solve Equation 1 for x and _____ the result in Equation 2.

$x = $ _____   **Solve Equation 1 for x.**

___ (_____) + ___ = ___   **Substitute for x in Equation 2.**

_____ + ___ = ___   **Simplify.**

$y = $ ___   **Solve for y.**

___ + ___ = ___   **Substitute for y in Equation 1.**

$x = $ ___   **Solve for x.**

Check Substitute in each equation to check your result.

Equation 1   **Equation 2**

___ + ___ = ___   ___ + ___ = ___

___ + ___ $\overset{?}{=}$ ___   ___ (___) + ___ (___) $\overset{?}{=}$ ___

___ = ___   ___ + ___ $\overset{?}{=}$ ___

                                           ___ = ___

Answer The health food store should include ____ pounds of granol and ___ pounds of raisins in the mixture.

✓ Checkpoint Choose a method to solve the linear system. Explain your choice, and then solve the system.

1. In Example 1, suppose the health food store wants to make 30 pounds of raisin granola that costs $125. How many pounds of granola and raisins do they need? Use the prices given in Example 1.

2. An owner of two stores buys five large delivery vans and five small delivery vans. One store receives three of the large delivery vans and two of the small delivery vans for a total cost of $161,000. The other store receives the rest of the vans for a total cost of $154,000. What is the cost of each type of van?

7.5 Special Types of Linear Systems

Goals
· Identify linear systems as having one solution, no solution, or infinitely many solutions.
· Model real-life problems.

Example 1   *A Linear System with No Solution*

Show that the linear system has no solution.

$-x + y = -3$ **Equation 1**

$-x + y = 2$ **Equation 2**

Solution

Method 1: **Graphing** Rewrite each equation in slope-intercept form. Then graph the linear system.

$y = $ _____   **Revised Equation 1**

$y = $ _____   **Revised Equation 2**

Answer Because the lines have the same slope but different *y*-intercepts, they are _____ . _____ lines do not _____ , so the system has _____ .

Method 2: **Substitution** Because Equation 2 can be rewritten as $y = $ _____ , you can substitute _____ for *y* in Equation 1.

$-x + y = -3$ **Write Equation 1.**

$-x + $ _____ $= -3$ **Substitute** _____ **for *y*.**

__ $= -3$ **Simplify.** _____ **statement**

Answer The variables are _____ and you are left with a statement that is _____ regardless of the values of *x* and *y*. This tells you that the system has _____ .

Example 2   *A Linear System with Many Solutions*

Show that the linear system has infinitely many solutions.

$3x + y = -1$ **Equation 1**

$-6x - 2y = 2$ **Equation 2**

Solution

Method 1: **Graphing** Rewrite each equation in slope-intercept form. Then graph the linear system.

$y = $ _____   **Revised Equation 1**

$y = $ _____   **Revised Equation 2**

Answer From these equations you can see that the equations represent the same line. _____ point on the line is a solution.

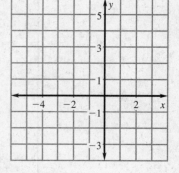

Method 2: **Linear Combinations** You can multiply Equation 1 by ___ .

___$x + $ ___$y = $ ____   **Multiply Equation 1 by** ___ .

$-6x - $ $2y = 2$ **Write Equation 2.**

___ $= $ ___   **Add equations.** _____ **statement**

Answer The variables are _____ and you are left with a statement that is _____ regardless of the values of x and y. This tells you that the system has _____ .

✓ *Checkpoint* **Use the substitution method or linear combination to solve the linear system and tell how many solutions the system has.**

1. $x - 2y = 3$

    $-5x + 10y = -15$

2. $-2x + 3y = 4$

    $-4x + 6y = 10$

3. $-25x + 15y = 2$

    $5x - 3y = 7$

4. $x + y = -6$

    $11x - y = 42$

7.6 Solving Systems of Linear Inequalities

Goals • Solve a system of linear inequalities by graphing.
• Use a system of linear inequalities to model a real-life situation.

VOCABULARY

System of linear inequalities

Solution of a system of linear inequalities

Graph of a system of linear inequalities

Example 1   A Triangular Solution Region

Graph the system of linear inequalities.

$y \geq -3$	**Inequality 1**
$x < 2$	**Inequality 2**
$y < x + 1$	**Inequality 3**

Solution

Graph all three inequalities in the same coordinate plane. The graph of the system is the overlap, or intersection, of the three half-planes.

To check your graph, choose a point in the overlap of the half-planes. Then substitute the coordinates into each inequality. If each inequality is true, then the point is a solution.

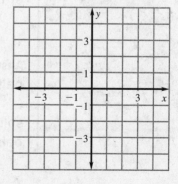

Example 2   *Solution Region Between Parallel Lines*

Write a system of inequalities that
defines the shaded region at the right.

Solution

The graph of one inequality is the half-
plane to the *left* of _____ .

The graph of the other inequality is the
half-plane to the *right* of _____ .

The shaded region of the graph is the
vertical band that lies _____ the two vertical lines, _____
and _____ , but not ____ the lines.

Answer The system of linear inequalities below defines the shaded
region.

_____ **Inequality 1**

_____ **Inequality 2**

Example 3   *A Quadrilateral Solution Region*

Graph the system of linear inequalities. Label each vertex of the solution region. Describe the shape of the region.	$x \geq 0$ **Inequality 1**
	$y \geq 0$ **Inequality 2**
	$y \leq 1$ **Inequality 3**
	$y \leq -x + 3$ **Inequality 4**

Solution

Graph all four inequalities in the same
coordinate plane. Then label the vertices
of the solution region.

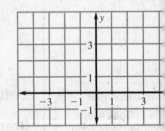

Answer The region that lies in all four
half-planes is a quadrilateral with vertices at (__ , __), (__ , __
(__ , __), and (__ , __). Note that (0, 3) is not a vertex of the
solution region even though two boundary lines intersect at that
point.

1. Graph the system of linear inequalities.

$$y < 2x + 2$$

$$y > -\frac{1}{2}x - 1$$

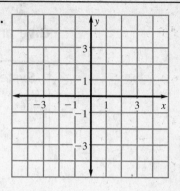

2. Write a system of linear inequalities that defines the shaded region.

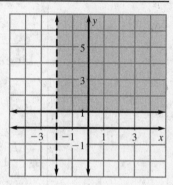

3. Graph the system of linear inequalities. Label each vertex of the solution region. Describe the shape of the region.

$$x \geq 0$$

$$y \leq 0$$

$$y \geq -3$$

$$y \geq x - 4$$

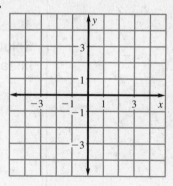

Words to Review

Give an example of the vocabulary word.

System of linear equations	Solution of a system of linear equations
Linear combination	System of linear inequalities
Solution of a system of linear inequalities	Graph of a system of linear inequalities

Review your notes and Chapter 7 by using the Chapter Review on pages 440–442 of your textbook.

Multiplication Properties of Exponents

Goals • Use properties of exponents to multiply exponential expressions.
  • Use powers to model real-life problems.

MULTIPLICATION PROPERTIES OF EXPONENTS

Let a and b be numbers and let m and n be positive integers.

Product of Powers Property
To multiply powers having the same base, _____.

$a^m \cdot a^n = $ _____   Example: $3^2 \cdot 3^7 = $ _____

Power of a Power Property
To find a power of a power, _____.

$(a^m)^n = $ _____   Example: $(5^2)^4 = $ _____

Power of a Product Property
To find a power of a product, _____

_____.

$(a \cdot b)^m = $ _____   Example: $(2 \cdot 3)^6 = $ _____

Example 1 *Using the Product of Powers Property*

a. $4^3 \cdot 4^5 = 4$_____   b. $y^4 \cdot y^5 \cdot y^6 = y$_____

  $= 4$__ $= y$__

c. $6^2 \cdot 6 = 6^2 \cdot 6$__   d. $(-3)(-3)^7 = (-3)$__ $\cdot (-3)^7$

  $= 6$_____ $= (-3)$_____

  $= 6$__ $= (-3)$__

Example 2 *Using the Power of a Power Property*

a. $(7^3)^5 = $ _____   b. $(x^2)^5 = $ _____

c. $[(-2)^4]^3 = $ _____

d. $[(b - 1)^6]^4 = $ _____

Example 3   *Using the Power of a Product Property*

a. $(2 \cdot 3)^3 = $ ___ $\cdot$ ___   **Raise each factor to a power.**

$= $ ___ $\cdot$ ___   **Evaluate each power.**

$= $ _____   **Multiply.**

b. $(9xy)^2 = (9 \cdot x \cdot y)^2$ **Identify factors.**

$= $ ___ $\cdot$ ___ $\cdot$ ___   **Raise each factor to a power.**

$= $ _____   **Simplify.**

c. $(-3z)^4 = ($ ___ $\cdot$ ___ $)^4$ _____

$= $ _____   _____

$= $ _____   _____

d. $-(4w)^3 = -(4 \cdot w)^3$ _____

$= $ _____   _____

$= $ _____   _____

Example 4   *Using All Three Properties*

Simplify $(7w^2z^3)^2 \cdot z^4$.

$(7w^2z^3)^2 \cdot z^4 = 7$___ $\cdot (w^2)$___ $\cdot (z^3)$___ $\cdot z^4$ **Power of a produ**

$= $ ___ $\cdot$ ___ $\cdot$ ___ $\cdot$ ___   **Power of a power**

$= $ _____   **Product of power**

✔ *Checkpoint* **Simplify the expression.**

1. $(-4)^3 \cdot (-4)^6$	**2.** $w^{10} \cdot w$	**3.** $(d^4)^5$
4. $(6p)^2$	**5.** $(-2xy)^4$	**6.** $(2wz^2)^5(wz)^2$

8.2 Zero and Negative Exponents

Goals • Evaluate powers that have zero and negative exponents.
• Graph exponential functions.

VOCABULARY

Exponential function

DEFINITION OF ZERO AND NEGATIVE EXPONENTS

Let a be a nonzero number and let n be a positive integer.

• A nonzero number to the zero power is 1: $a^0 = 1$, $a \neq 0$.

• a^{-n} is the reciprocal of a^n: $a^{-n} = \dfrac{1}{a^n}$, $a \neq 0$.

Example 1   *Powers with Zero and Negative Exponents*

a. $4^{-2} = \underline{\quad} = \underline{\quad}$ 4^{-2} is the reciprocal of ___.

b. $(-5)^0 = \underline{\quad}$ a^0 is __.

c. $7^{-y} = \dfrac{\quad}{\quad}$ 7^{-y} is the reciprocal of ___.

d. $\left(\dfrac{1}{9}\right)^{-1} = \underline{\quad}$ The reciprocal of $\dfrac{1}{9}$ is __.

e. $0^{-2} = \underline{\qquad\qquad}$ Zero has \underline{\qquad\qquad}.

Example 2 *Simplifying Exponential Expressions*

Rewrite with positive exponents.

a. $7(4^{-y})$ **b.** $3x^{-4}y^{-5}$ **c.** $(6d)^{-2}$ **d.** $\dfrac{1}{c^{-2}}$

Solution

a. $7(4^{-y}) = \underline{\hspace{1cm}} = \underline{\hspace{1cm}}$

b. $3x^{-4}y^{-5} = 3 \cdot \underline{\hspace{1cm}} \cdot \underline{\hspace{1cm}} = \underline{\hspace{1.5cm}}$

c. $(6d)^{-2} = 6\underline{\hspace{0.5cm}} \cdot d\underline{\hspace{0.5cm}} = \underline{\hspace{1cm}} \cdot \underline{\hspace{1cm}} = \underline{\hspace{1.5cm}}$

d. $\dfrac{1}{c^{-2x}} = (c^{-2x})^{-1} = c\underline{\hspace{2cm}} = \underline{\hspace{1cm}}$

Example 3 *Evaluating Exponential Expressions*

Evaluate the expression.

a. $2^4 \cdot 2^{-4}$ **b.** $(3^{-2})^{-2}$ **c.** 2^{-6}

Solution

a. $2^4 \cdot 2^{-4} = 2\underline{\hspace{1.5cm}}$ Use \underline{\hspace{2cm}} prope

$= 2\underline{\hspace{0.5cm}}$ \underline{\hspace{1cm}} exponents.

$= \underline{\hspace{0.5cm}}$ $a\underline{\hspace{0.3cm}}$ is $\underline{\hspace{0.3cm}}$.

b. $(3^{-2})^{-2} = 3\underline{\hspace{1.5cm}}$ Use \underline{\hspace{2cm}} proper

$= 3\underline{\hspace{0.5cm}}$ \underline{\hspace{1.5cm}} exponents.

$= \underline{\hspace{0.5cm}}$ Evaluate.

c. $2^{-6} = \underline{\hspace{1cm}}$ Write reciprocal of $\underline{\hspace{0.5cm}}$.

$= \underline{\hspace{1cm}}$ Evaluate.

$= \underline{\hspace{1.5cm}}$ Use a calculator.

✔ *Checkpoint* Evaluate the exponential expression. Write fractions in simplest form.

1. 2^{-5}	2. 4^{-3}	3. $\left(\dfrac{1}{7}\right)^{-1}$	4. $15\left(\dfrac{1}{5}\right)^{-1}$
5. $-12^0 \cdot \dfrac{1}{5^{-2}}$	6. $3 \cdot 3^{-3}$	7. $13^0 \cdot 0^{-2}$	8. $15^{-1} \cdot 15$

Rewrite the expression with positive exponents.

9. a^{-6}	10. $\dfrac{1}{3y^{-4}}$	11. $(2x^{-2}y)^3$	12. $\left(\dfrac{-3x^3}{6x^{-2}}\right)^{-1}$

Example 4   *Graphing an Exponential Function*

Graph the exponential function $y = 3^x$.

Solution

Make a table that includes negative *x*-values.

x	−2	−1	0	1	2
3^x					

Draw a coordinate plane and plot the five points given by the table.

Then draw a smooth curve through the points.

Notice the graph has a *y*-intercept of ___, and that it gets closer to the _____ side of the *x*-axis as the _____ get smaller.

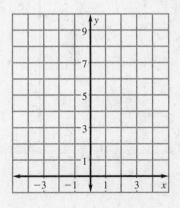

Division Properties of Exponents

Goals • Use the division properties of exponents to evaluate powers and simplify expressions.
• Use the division properties of exponents to find a probability.

DIVISION PROPERTIES OF EXPONENTS

Let a and b be numbers and let m and n be integers.

Quotient of Powers Property
To divide powers having the same base, _____ exponents.

$$\frac{a^m}{a^n} = \underline{\qquad}, a \neq 0 \qquad \textbf{Example: } \frac{3^7}{3^5} = \underline{\qquad} = \underline{\quad}$$

Power of a Quotient Property
To find a power of a quotient, find the power of the numerator and the power of the denominator and _____.

$$\left(\frac{a}{b}\right)^m = \underline{\quad}, b \neq 0 \qquad \textbf{Example: } \left(\frac{4}{5}\right)^3 = \underline{\quad}$$

Example 1 *Using the Quotient of Powers Property*

a. $\dfrac{8^4}{8^3} = 8\underline{\qquad}$

$= 8\underline{\quad}$

$= \underline{\quad}$

b. $\dfrac{(-7)^5}{(-7)^5} = (-7)\underline{\qquad}$

$= (-7)\underline{\quad}$

$= \underline{\quad}$

c. $\dfrac{5^3 \cdot 5}{5^5} = \dfrac{5\underline{\quad}}{5^5}$

$= 5\underline{\qquad}$

$= 5\underline{\quad}$

$= \underline{\quad}$

d. $\dfrac{1}{x^7} \cdot x^4 = \underline{\quad}$

$= x\underline{\qquad}$

$= x\underline{\quad}$

$= \underline{\quad}$

Example 2   *Using the Power of a Quotient Property*

Simplify the expression $\left(-\dfrac{8}{5}\right)^{-3}$.

$$\left(-\dfrac{8}{5}\right)^{-3} = \left(\dfrac{-8}{5}\right)^{-3}$$ Rewrite fraction.

$$= \underline{\hspace{3cm}}$$ Power of a quotient

$$= \underline{\hspace{2cm}}$$ Definition of negative exponents

$$= \underline{\hspace{4cm}}$$ Simplify.

Example 3   *Simplifying Expressions*

Simplify the expression.

a. $\dfrac{3xy^4}{4x^3} \cdot \dfrac{12x^3y^2}{x^2}$ b. $\left(\dfrac{2x^2}{y^3}\right)^5$

Solution

a. $\dfrac{3xy^4}{4x^3} \cdot \dfrac{12x^3y^2}{x^2} = \dfrac{(3xy^4)(12x^3y^2)}{(4x^3)(x^2)}$ Multiply fractions.

$$= \underline{\hspace{3cm}}$$ Product of powers

$$= \underline{\hspace{2cm}}$$ Quotient of powers

$$= \underline{\hspace{1.5cm}}$$ Product of powers

b. $\left(\dfrac{2x^2}{y^3}\right)^5 = \underline{\hspace{2.5cm}}$ Power of a quotient

$$= \underline{\hspace{3cm}}$$ Power of a quotient

$$= \underline{\hspace{2cm}}$$ Simplify.

✔ Checkpoint Evaluate the expression. Write fractions in simple form.

1. $\dfrac{4^7}{4^4}$	2. $\dfrac{(-7)^8}{-7^8}$	3. $\dfrac{2^2}{2^{-8}}$	4. $\left(\dfrac{3}{4}\right)^4$

Simplify the expression. The simplified expression should have no negative exponents.

5. $\left(\dfrac{2}{y^2}\right)^6$	6. $x^5 \cdot \dfrac{2}{x^{11}}$	7. $\dfrac{5x^2y^3}{6x^4} \cdot \dfrac{24x^5y^2}{x^6y^3}$

8.4 Scientific Notation

Goals • Use scientific notation to represent numbers.
• Use scientific notation to describe real-life situations.

VOCABULARY

Scientific notation _____

Example 1   *Rewriting in Decimal Form*

Rewrite in decimal form.   **a.** 7.29×10^6 **b.** 4.5×10^{-7}

Solution

a. $7.29 \times 10^6 = $ _____   **Move decimal point** _____.

b. $4.5 \times 10^{-7} = $ _____   **Move decimal point** _____.

✔ *Checkpoint* **Rewrite in decimal form.**

1. 2.49×10^5	**2.** 9.6×10^{-3}	**3.** 4.00027×10^7

Example 2   *Rewriting in Scientific Notation*

a. $618 = $ _____ $\times 10$__   **Move decimal point** _____ **places.**

b. $2.5 = $ ___ $\times 10$__   **Move decimal point** _____.

c. $0.00007245 = $ _____   **Move decimal point** _____.

d. $310{,}000{,}000 = $ _____   **Move decimal point** _____.

✓ *Checkpoint* **Rewrite in scientific notation.**

4. 0.006	5. 800,200,000,000	6. 0.0000037

Example 3 *Computing with Scientific Notation*

Evaluate the expression. Write the result in scientific notation.

a. $(6.0 \times 10^3)(2.4 \times 10^5)$ **b.** $(3.0 \times 10^{-4})^3$

c. $(5.4 \times 10^{-2}) \div (7.2 \times 10^{-8})$

Solution

a. $(6.0 \times 10^3)(2.4 \times 10^5)$

$= ($ ___ $\cdot$ ___ $) \times ($ ___ $\cdot$ ___ $)$ Associative prope of multiplication

$=$ _____   Simplify.

$=$ _____   Write in scientific notation.

b. $(3.0 \times 10^{-4})^3 =$ _____   Power of a produc

$=$ _____   Power of a power

$=$ _____   Write in scientific notation.

c. $\dfrac{5.4 \times 10^{-2}}{7.2 \times 10^{-8}} =$ ___ $\times$ ___   Rewrite as a prod

$=$ _____   Simplify.

$=$ _____   Write in scientific notation.

✓ *Checkpoint* **Evaluate the expression without using a calculato Write the result in scientific notation and in decimal form.**

7. $(2.5 \times 10^4)(4.1 \times 10^6)$	8. $(2.4 \times 10^{-4}) \div (9.6 \times 10^-$

8.5 Exponential Growth Functions

Goals • Write and use models for exponential growth.
• Graph models for exponential growth.

VOCABULARY

Exponential growth

EXPONENTIAL GROWTH MODEL

C is the **initial amount.**   *t* is the **time period.**

$$y = C(1 + r)^t$$

$(1 + r)$ is the **growth factor,** *r* is the **growth rate.**

The **percent of increase is 100***r*.

Example 1 *Finding the Balance in an Account*

Compound Interest You deposit $450 in an account that pays 2.5% annual interest compounded yearly. What is the account balance after 10 years?

Solution *Method 1:* **Solve a Simpler Problem**

Find the account balance A_1 after 1 year and multiply by the growth factor to find the balance for each of the following years. The growth rate is _____ , so the growth factor is _____.

$A_1 = 450(1.025) = $ _____   **Balance after 1 year**

$A_2 = 450(1.025)(1.025) \approx $ _____   **Balance after 2 years**

$A_3 = 450(1.025)(1.025)(1.025) \approx $ _____   **Balance after 3 years**

$\vdots$

$A_{10} = 450(1.025)^{10} \approx $ _____   **Balance after 10 years**

Answer The balance after 10 years will be about $ _____ .

Example 2   *Using a Formula*

Use the exponential growth model to find the account balance
in Example 1.

The growth rate is _____. The initial value is _____.

$A = C(1 + r)^t$ **Exponential growth mode**

$= \underline{\quad}(1 + \underline{\quad})\underline{\quad}$ **Substitute for C, r, and t**

$= \underline{\qquad\qquad}$ **Simplify.**

$\approx \underline{\qquad}$ **Evaluate.**

Answer The balance after 10 years will be about $_____.

Example 3   *Writing an Exponential Growth Model*

Population Growth A population of 25 mice doubles each year
4 years.

a. What is the percent of increase each year?

b. What is the population after 4 years?

Solution

a. The population doubles each year, so the growth factor is 2.

$1 + r = 2$

Answer So, the growth rate is 1 and the percent of increase ea**
year is 100%.

b. After 4 years, the population can be found as follows.

$P = C(1 + r)^t$ **Exponential growth model**

$= \underline{\qquad\qquad}$ **Substitute for C, r, and t.**

$= \underline{\qquad}$ **Simplify.**

$= \underline{\quad}$ **Evaluate.**

Answer There will be about _____ mice after 4 years.

Checkpoint Complete the following exercises.

---

1. You deposit $375 in an account that pays 3.0% annual interest compounded yearly. What is the account balance after 10 years?

---

2. A company starts with 20 employees and after one year it has 30. The company increases employees at the same rate every year for 6 years.

a. What is the percent of increase each year?

b. What is the population after 6 years?

Exponential Decay Functions

Goals • Write and use models for exponential decay.
• Graph models for exponential decay.

VOCABULARY

Exponential decay

EXPONENTIAL DECAY MODEL

C is the **initial amount.** t is the **time period.**

$$y = C(1 - r)^t$$

$(1 - r)$ is the **decay factor,**
r is the **decay rate.** To assure
$1 > (1 - r) > 0$, it is
necessary that $0 < r < 1$.

The **percent of decrease is** $100r$.

Example 1   *Writing an Exponential Decay Model*

Depreciation A car is purchased for $20,000. The value of the car will be less each year because of depreciation. The car depreciates (loses value) at the rate of 25% per year. Write an exponential decay model to represent this situation.

Solution

The initial value C is $\$$_____. The decay rate r is _____. Let y b
the value of the car in dollars and let t be the age of the car in years.

$y = C(1 - r)^t$ **Exponential decay model**

$y = $ _____$(1 - $ _____$)^t$ **Substitute for C and r.**

$y = $ _____$($ _____$)^t$ **Simplify.**

Answer The exponential decay model is $y = $ _____.

Example 2 *Using an Exponential Decay Model*

Use the model in Example 1 to estimate the value of the car in 5 years.

To find the value in 5 years, substitute 5 for *t*.

$y =$ _____(_____)^t **Exponential decay model**

$=$ _____   **Substitute for *t*.**

$\approx$ _____   **Use a calculator.**

Answer According to this model, the value of the car in 5 years will be about $_____.

✓ *Checkpoint* **Complete the following exercises.**

1. Verify the model you found in Example 1. Find the value of the car for each year by multiplying the value in the previous year by the decay factor.

Year	Value

2. A used boat costs $3200. The value of the boat will be less each year because of depreciation. The boat depreciates at the rate of 13% per year.

   a. Write an exponential decay model to represent this situation.

   b. Estimate the value of the boat in 3 years.

Example 3 | *Graphing an Exponential Decay Model*

a. Graph the exponential decay model in Example 1.

b. Use the graph to estimate the value of the car in 8 years.

Solution

a. Use the table of values in Checkpoint 1. Plot the points in a coordinate plane. Then, draw a smooth curve through the points.

b. From the graph, the value of your car in 8 years will be about $_____.

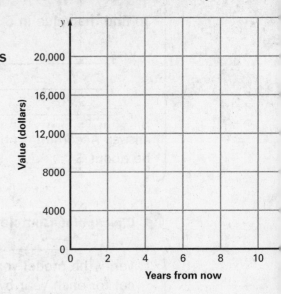

✔ Checkpoint Complete the following exercise.

3. a. Graph the exponential decay model in Checkpoint 2.

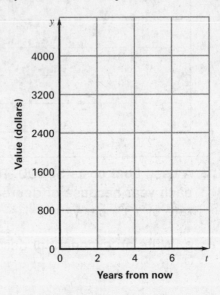

b. Estimate the value of the boat in 5 years.

Words to Review

Give an example of the vocabulary word.

Exponential function	Scientific notation
Exponential growth	Growth factor
Initial amount	Time period
Percent of increase	Growth rate
Exponential decay	Decay factor
Decay rate	Percent of decrease

Review your notes and Chapter 8 by using the Chapter Review on pages 494–496 of your textbook.

Solving Quadratic Equations by Finding Square Roots

Goals • Evaluate and approximate square roots.
• Solve a quadratic equation by finding square roots.

VOCABULARY

Positive square root

Negative square root

Radicand

Perfect squares

Irrational number

Radical expression

Quadratic equation in standard form

Leading coefficient

Example 1 **Finding Square Roots of Numbers**

Evaluate the expression.

a. $-\sqrt{49}$ b. $\sqrt{49}$ c. $\sqrt{-9}$ d. $\sqrt{0}$

Solution

a. $-\sqrt{49}$ _____   _____ square root

b. $\sqrt{49}$ _____   _____ square root

c. $\sqrt{-9}$ _____   _____ square root

d. $\sqrt{0}$ _____   _____

Example 2   **Evaluating a Radical Expression**

Evaluate $\sqrt{b^2 - 4ac}$ when $a = -7$, $b = 8$, and $c = -1$.

$\sqrt{b^2 - 4ac} = \sqrt{\underline{} - 4(\underline{})(\underline{})}$ **Substitute values.**

$= \sqrt{\underline{} - \underline{}}$ **Simplify.**

$= \sqrt{\underline{}}$ **Simplify.**

$= \underline{}$ **Positive square root**

✔ **Checkpoint** **Find all square roots of the number or write no square roots.**

1. 81	2. -64	3. 121	4. 0.49

Evaluate $\sqrt{b^2 - 4ac}$ for the given values.

5. $a = 2$, $b = -3$, $c = -2$	6. $a = 4$, $b = 9$, $c = 2$

Example 3 Solving Quadratic Equations

Solve each equation.

a. $x^2 = 6$ **b.** $x^2 = 144$ **c.** $x^2 = -7$

Solution

a. $x^2 = 6$ has two solutions: $x =$ _____ and $x =$ _____.

b. $x^2 = 144$ has two solutions: $x =$ ___ and $x =$ ____.

c. $x^2 = -7$ has _____.

Example 4 Rewriting Before Finding Square Roots

Solve $5x^2 - 20 = 0$.

$5x^2 - 20 = 0$	Write original equation.
$5x^2 =$ ____	Add ____ to each side.
$x^2 =$ ____	Divide each side by ___.
$x =$ _____	Find square roots.
$x =$ ____	____ is a perfect square.

✔ **Checkpoint** Solve the equation or write *no solution*.

7. $x^2 = 11$	8. $3x^2 - 75 = 0$	9. $2x^2 - 22 = 50$

9.2 Simplifying Radicals

Goals
- Use properties of radicals to simplify radicals.
- Use quadratic equations to model real-life problems.

VOCABULARY

Simplest form

PROPERTIES OF RADICALS

Product Property The square root of a product equals the product of the _____ of the factors.

$$\sqrt{ab} = \underline{\quad} \cdot \underline{\quad} \text{ where } a \geq 0 \text{ and } b \geq 0$$

Quotient Property The square root of a quotient equals the quotient of the square roots of the _____ and

_____ .

$$\sqrt{\frac{a}{b}} = \frac{\underline{\quad}}{\underline{\quad}} \text{ when } a \geq 0 \text{ and } b \geq 0$$

Example 1 *Simplifying with the Product Property*

Simplify the expression $\sqrt{27}$.

Solution

You can use the product property to simplify a radical by removing perfect square factors from the radicand.

$$\sqrt{27} = \sqrt{\underline{\quad}} \qquad \text{Factor using perfect square factor.}$$

$$= \sqrt{\underline{\quad}} \cdot \sqrt{\underline{\quad}} \qquad \text{Use product property.}$$

$$= \underline{\quad} \qquad \text{Simplify.}$$

Example 2   *Simplifying with the Quotient Property*

Simplify the expression.

a. $\sqrt{\dfrac{5}{16}}$ 　　　　　　　　　b. $\sqrt{\dfrac{48}{75}}$

Solution

a. $\sqrt{\dfrac{5}{16}} = \dfrac{}{}$ Use quotient property.

$= \dfrac{}{}$ Simplify.

b. $\sqrt{\dfrac{48}{75}} = \sqrt{\dfrac{}{}}$ Factor using perfect square factors

$= \sqrt{}$ Divide out common factors.

$= \dfrac{}{}$ Use quotient property.

$= \dfrac{}{}$ Simplify.

✔ *Checkpoint* Simplify the expression.

1. $\sqrt{12}$	2. $\sqrt{63}$	3. $\sqrt{\dfrac{13}{36}}$
4. $\sqrt{\dfrac{48}{81}}$	5. $\dfrac{\sqrt{54}}{3}$	6. $\sqrt{\dfrac{90}{160}}$

9.3 Graphing Quadratic Functions

Goals • Sketch the graph of a quadratic function.
• Use quadratic models in real-life settings.

VOCABULARY

Quadratic function in standard form

Parabola

Vertex of a parabola

Axis of symmetry of a parabola

GRAPH OF A QUADRATIC FUNCTION

The graph of $y = ax^2 + bx + c$ is a _____.

• If a is positive, the parabola opens ___.

• If a is negative, the parabola opens _____.

• The _____ has an x-coordinate of $-\dfrac{b}{2a}$.

• The _____ is the vertical line $x = -\dfrac{b}{2a}$.

Example 1   *Graphing a Quadratic Function*

Sketch the graph of $y = x^2 - 4x + 4$.

Find the *x*-coordinate of the vertex when $a = $ ___ and $b = $ _____.

$$-\frac{b}{2a} = \underline{\hspace{2cm}} = \underline{\hspace{0.7cm}}$$

Make a table of values, using *x*-values to the left and right of $x = $ ___.

x	−1	0	1	2	3	4	5
y							

Plot the points. The vertex is (___ , ___) and the axis of symmetry is $x = $ ___. Connect the points to form a parabola that opens ____ because *a* is _____.

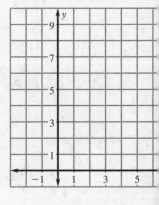

Example 2   *Graphing a Quadratic Function*

Sketch the graph of $y = -x^2 + 2x - 1$.

Find the *x*-coordinate of the vertex when $a = $ _____ and $b = $ ___.

$$-\frac{b}{2a} = \underline{\hspace{2cm}} = \underline{\hspace{0.7cm}}$$

Make a table of values, using *x*-values to the left and right of $x = $ ___.

x	−2	−1	0	1	2	3	4
y							

Plot the points. The vertex is (___ , ___) and the axis of symmetry is $x = $ ___. Connect the points to form a parabola that opens _____ because *a* is _____.

Checkpoint Tell whether the graph opens up or down. Write an equation of the axis of symmetry.

1. $y = -x^2 - x + 1$	2. $y = 3x^2 - 2x + 2$

Sketch the graph of the quadratic function. Label the vertex.

3. $y = x^2 + 2x - 5$	4. $y = -4x^2 + 4x - 1$
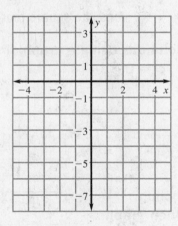	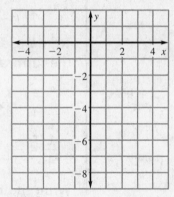

9.4 Solving Quadratic Equations by Graphing

Goals • Solve a quadratic equation graphically.
• Use quadratic models in real-life settings.

VOCABULARY

Roots

Example 1 *Representing a Solution Using a Graph*

Solve $\frac{1}{4}x^2 = 9$ algebraically. Represent your solutions as the
x-intercepts of a graph.

Solution

$\frac{1}{4}x^2 = 9$ **Write original equation.**

$x^2 = \underline{\hspace{1cm}}$ **Multiply each side by ___ .**

$x = \underline{\hspace{1cm}}$ **Find the square root of each side.**

To represent these solutions using a graph, first write the equation
the form $ax^2 + bx + c = 0$.

$\frac{1}{4}x^2 = 9$

$\frac{1}{4}x^2 - \underline{\hspace{0.7cm}} = \underline{\hspace{0.7cm}}$

Write the related function
$y = ax^2 + bx + c$. Then graph
the function.

$y = \underline{\hspace{2cm}}$

The x-intercepts are ____ , which
are the algebraic solutions.

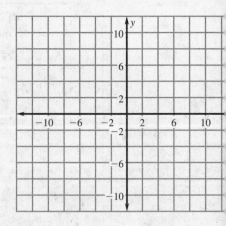

Example 2   *Solving an Equation Graphically*

Solve $x^2 + 2x = 3$ graphically. Check your solution algebraically.

Solution

Write the equation in the form $ax^2 + bx + c = 0$.

$x^2 + 2x = 3$ Write the original equation.

$x^2 + 2x \underline{\hspace{1cm}} = \underline{\hspace{0.5cm}}$ Subtract ___ from each side.

Write the related function $y = ax^2 + bx + c$.

$y = \underline{\hspace{3cm}}$

Sketch the graph of the function $y = \underline{\hspace{3cm}}$.

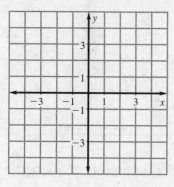

From the graph, the x-intercepts appear to be $x = \underline{\hspace{1cm}}$ and $x = \underline{\hspace{0.5cm}}$.

Check You can check this by using substitution.

            Check $x = \underline{\hspace{1cm}}$ Check $x = \underline{\hspace{0.5cm}}$

            $x^2 + 2x = 3$ $x^2 + 2x = 3$

$(\underline{\hspace{1cm}})^2 + 2(\underline{\hspace{1cm}}) \stackrel{?}{=} 3$ $(\underline{\hspace{0.5cm}})^2 + 2(\underline{\hspace{0.5cm}}) \stackrel{?}{=} 3$

                $\underline{\hspace{1.5cm}} \stackrel{?}{=} 3$ $\underline{\hspace{1.5cm}} \stackrel{?}{=} 3$

                $\underline{\hspace{1cm}} = 3$ $\underline{\hspace{1cm}} = 3$

✔ Checkpoint Solve the equation algebraically. Check the
solutions graphically.

---

1. $\dfrac{1}{16}x^2 = 4$

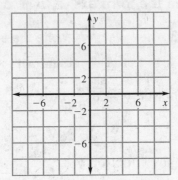

2. $-\dfrac{1}{3}x^2 = -3$

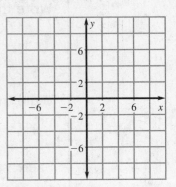

**Represent the solution graphically. Check the solution
algebraically.**

---

3. $x^2 - 2x = 8$

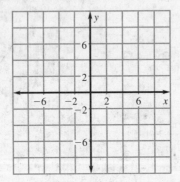

4. $x^2 + 4x = 5$

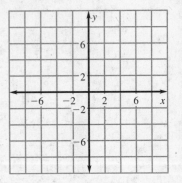

Solving Quadratic Equations by the Quadratic Formula

Goals • Use the quadratic formula to solve a quadratic equation.
• Use quadratic models for real-life situations.

THE QUADRATIC FORMULA

The solutions of the quadratic equation $ax^2 + bx + c = 0$ are

$$x = \frac{-\underline{} \pm \sqrt{\underline{} - 4\underline{}\underline{}}}{2\underline{}} \quad \text{when } \underline{} \neq \underline{} \text{ and}$$

$$\underline{} \geq \underline{}.$$

Example 1 *Using the Quadratic Formula*

Solve $x^2 + 8x + 15 = 0$ by using the quadratic formula.

(1)$x^2 + 8x + 15 = 0$ Identify $a = \underline{}$, $b = \underline{}$, and $c = \underline{}$.

$$x = \frac{-\underline{} \pm \sqrt{\underline{} - 4\underline{}}}{2\underline{}} \quad\quad \text{Write quadratic formula.}$$

$$= \frac{-\underline{} \pm \sqrt{\underline{} - 4(\underline{})(\underline{})}}{2(\underline{})} \quad\quad \text{Substitute values in the quadratic formula.}$$

$$= \frac{-\underline{} \pm \sqrt{\underline{} - \underline{}}}{\underline{}} \quad\quad \text{Simplify.}$$

$$= \frac{-\underline{} \pm \sqrt{\underline{}}}{\underline{}} \quad\quad \text{Simplify.}$$

$$= \underline{} \quad\quad \text{Solutions}$$

Answer The equation has two solutions:

$$x = \underline{} = \underline{} \text{ and } x = \underline{} = \underline{}.$$

Example 2 *Writing in Standard Form*

Solve $3x^2 - 7x = 11$.

Write the equation in standard form before using the quadratic formula.

$$3x^2 - 7x = 11$$ Write original equation.

$$3x^2 - 7x - 11 = 0$$ Rewrite equation in standard form.

$$x = \underline{\hspace{5cm}}$$ Write quadratic formula.

$$= \underline{\hspace{5cm}}$$ Substitute values into the quadratric formula: $a =$ ___ $b =$ ___, and $c =$ ___

$$= \underline{\hspace{5cm}}$$ Simplify.

$$= \underline{\hspace{5cm}}$$ Solutions

Answer The equation has two solutions:

$x = \underline{\hspace{2.5cm}} \approx \underline{\hspace{1.5cm}}$ and $x = \underline{\hspace{2.5cm}} \approx \underline{\hspace{1.5cm}}$.

✔ *Checkpoint* Use the quadratic formula to solve the equation.

1. $x^2 + 4x - 5 = 0$	2. $3x^2 - 8x = 9$

Example 3 *Modeling Vertical Motion*

Diving A cliff diver jumps from a height of 58 feet above the water with an initial velocity of 5 feet per second. How long will it take the diver to reach the water?

Solution

The diver's initial velocity is $v =$ _____ and the diver's initial height is $s =$ _____. The diver will reach the water when the height is _____.

$h = -16t^2$ _____   Choose a vertical motion model.

$h = -16t^2$ _____   Substitute values.

___ $= -16t^2$ _____   Substitute ___ for h. Write in standard form.

$t =$
_____   Write quadratic formula.

$=$
_____   Substitute values a, b, and c into quadratic formula.

$=$
_____   Simplify.

$\approx$ _____ or _____   Solutions

Answer Because time cannot be a negative number, disregard the solution of _____. So, the diver will reach the water in about _____ seconds.

✔ *Checkpoint* **Complete the following exercise.**

3. A tennis ball is dropped from the top of a building, which is 40 feet above the ground. How long will it take the tennis ball to reach the ground?

9.6 Applications of the Discriminant

Goals
- Use the discriminant to find the number of solutions of a quadratic equation.
- Apply the discriminant to solve real-life problems.

VOCABULARY

Discriminant

THE NUMBER OF SOLUTIONS OF A QUADRATIC EQUATION

Consider the quadratic equation $ax^2 + bx + c = 0$.

- If $b^2 - 4ac$ is positive, then the equation has

  _____ .

- If $b^2 - 4ac$ is zero, then the equation has _____ .

- If $b^2 - 4ac$ is negative, then the equation has

  _____ .

Example 1   *Finding the Number of Solutions*

Find the value of the discriminant and use the value to tell if the equation $x^2 - 2x - 9 = 0$ has *two solutions*, *one solution*, or *no real solution*.

Solution

$$b^2 - 4ac = (\underline{})^2 - 4(\underline{})(\underline{})$$ **Substitute for *a*, *b*, and *c*.**

$$= \underline{} + \underline{}$$ **Simplify.**

$$= \underline{}$$ **Discriminant is** _____

The discriminant is _____ , so the equation has

_____ .

Example 2   *Finding the Number of Solutions*

Find the value of the discriminant and use the value to tell if the equation has *two solutions, one solution,* or *no real solution.*

a. $x^2 - 8x + 16 = 0$ **b.** $-3x^2 + 4x - 5 = 0$

Solution

a. $b^2 - 4ac = (\underline{})^2 - 4(\underline{})(\underline{})$ _____

_____

$= \underline{} - \underline{}$ _____

$= \underline{}$ _____

The discriminant is _____, so the equation has _____.

b. $b^2 - 4ac = $ _____   _____

$= $ _____   _____

$= $ _____   _____

The discriminant is _____, so the equation has _____.

✔ *Checkpoint* **Tell if the** *equation* **has** *two solutions, one solution,* **or** *no real solution.*

1. $-x^2 - 5x - 9 = 0$	2. $4x^2 - 4x + 1 = 0$
3. $8x^2 + 8x + 1 = 0$	4. $-2x^2 + 3x - 5$

Example 3   *Finding the Number of x-Intercepts*

Use the related equation to find the number of x-intercepts of the graph of the function.

a. $y = x^2 - 2x - 1$ **b.** $y = x^2 - 2x + 3$

Solution

For each function, let $y = 0$. Then find the value of the discriminan

a. $b^2 - 4ac = ($ ___ $)^2 - 4($ __ $)($ ___ $)$ $a =$ __ , $b =$ ____ ,

                                         $c =$ ____

          $=$ __ $+$ __   **Simplify.**

          $=$ __   **Discriminant is** ____

The discriminant is _____ , so the equation has
_____ *and* the graph has _____ .

b. $b^2 - 4ac = ($ ___ $)^2 - 4($ __ $)($ __ $)$ _____

          $=$ __ $-$ __   _____

          $=$ ___   _____

                                              _____

The discriminant is _____ , so the equation has
_____ and the graph has _____ .

✔ **Checkpoint** Find the number of x-intercepts of the graph of the
function.

5. $y = x^2 - 2x + 1$	**6.** $y = x^2 - 4x + 5$	**7.** $y = 3x^2 - 6x +$

Graphing Quadratic Inequalities

Goals • Sketch the graph of a quadratic inequality.
 • Use quadratic inequalities as real-life models.

VOCABULARY

Quadratic inequalities

_____

Graph of a quadratic inequality

Example 1 *Checking Points*

Sketch the graph of $y = x^2 + 2x - 3$. Plot and label the points
$A(0, 1)$, $B(-2, 3)$, and $C(1, -3)$. Tell whether each point lies inside or
outside the parabola.

Solution

1. Sketch the graph of
   $y = x^2 + 2x - 3$.

2. Plot and label the points
   $A(0, 1)$, $B(-2, 3)$, and $C(1, -3)$.

   ___ and ___ lie inside the
   parabola while ___ lies outside.

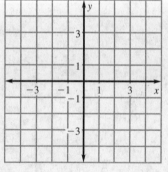

✔ *Checkpoint* Use the graph from Example 1 and tell whether the
point lies inside or outside the parabola.

1. (2, 1)	**2.** (−3, 4)	**3.** (−1, 2)	**4.** (−2, −4)

SKETCHING THE GRAPH OF A QUADRATIC INEQUALITY

Step 1 Sketch the graph of the equation $y = ax^2 + bx + c$ that corresponds to the inequality. Sketch a _____ parabola for inequalities with < or > to show that the points on the parabola are _____. Sketch a _____ parabola for inequalities with ≤ or ≥ to show that the points on the parabola are _____.

Step 2 The parabola you drew separates the coordinate plane into two regions. Test a point that is not on the parabola to find whether it is a solution of the inequality.

Step 3 If the test point is a solution, shade its region. If not, shade the other region.

Example 2 *Graphing a Quadratic Inequality*

Sketch the graph of $y < x^2 - 4x$.

Solution

1. Use the grid given below to sketch the equation $y = x^2 - 4x$ that corresponds to the inequality $y < x^2 - 4x$. Use a _____ line because the inequality is <. The parabola opens ____.

2. Test a point that is not on the parabola, say (0, 1).

   $y < x^2 - 4x$ **Write original inequality.**

   $\underline{\quad} \overset{?}{<} \underline{\quad}^2 - 4(\underline{\quad})$ **Substitute for x and y.**

   _____

   Because _____, the ordered pair (0, 1) _____.

3. The point (0, 1) _____ a solution and it is _____ the parabola, so the graph of $y < x^2 - 4x$ is all points _____, _____, the parabola.

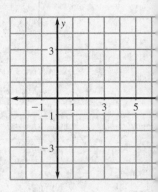

Example 3 *Graphing a Quadratic Inequality*

Sketch the graph of $y < -x^2 - 2x + 3$.

Solution

1. Use the grid given below to sketch the equation $y = -x^2 - 2x + 3$ that corresponds to the inequality $y \leq -x^2 - 2x + 3$. Use a _____ line because the inequality is $\leq$. The parabola opens _____.

2. Test a point that is not on the parabola, say (0, 0).

   $y \leq -x^2 - 2x + 3$ **Write original inequality.**

   $\underline{\hspace{1cm}} \overset{?}{\leq} -(\underline{\hspace{0.5cm}})^2 - 2(\underline{\hspace{0.5cm}}) + 3$ **Substitute for x and y.**

   _____   _____

   Because ____ less than or equal to ___, the ordered pair (0, 0) ___ a solution.

3. The point (0, 0) ___ a solution and it is _____ the parabola, so the graph of $y \leq -x^2 - 2x + 3$ is all points _____ parabola.

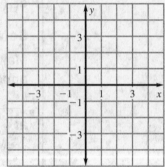

✔ *Checkpoint* **Sketch the graph of the inequality.**

5. $y > -x^2 + 4$	6. $y \geq x^2 - 4x + 3$
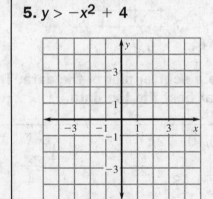	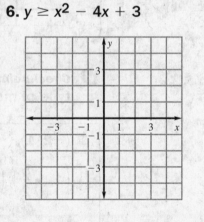

9.8 Comparing Linear, Exponential, and Quadratic Models

Goals • Choose a model that best fits a collection of data.
• Use models in real-life settings.

Example 1 **Choosing a Model**

Name the type of model that best fits each data collection.

a. $\left(-2, \frac{3}{2}\right), \left(-1, \frac{7}{4}\right), (0, 2), \left(1, \frac{9}{4}\right), \left(2, \frac{5}{2}\right)$

b. $\left(-2, \frac{1}{4}\right), \left(-1, \frac{1}{2}\right), (0, 1), (1, 2), (2, 4)$

c. $(-2, 1), (-1, 4), (0, 5), (1, 4), (2, 1)$

Solution

Make scatter plots of the data. Then decide whether the points appear to lie on a line (_____ model), an exponential curve (_____ model), or a parabola (_____ model).

a. _____
   Model

b. _____
   Model

c. _____
   Model

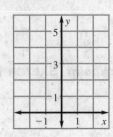

✔ **Checkpoint** Make a scatter plot of the data. Then name the type of model that best fits the data.

1. $(-2, 1), (-1, -1), (0, -2),$
$\left(1, -\frac{5}{2}\right), \left(2, -\frac{11}{4}\right), \left(3, -\frac{23}{8}\right)$

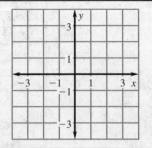

Example 2   *Writing a Model*

Population Growth The population *p* of fruit flies after *d* days is shown in the table below. Decide which type of model best fits the data. Write a model.

Days, *d*	0	1	2	3	4
Population, *p*	32	48	72	108	162

Solution

Draw a scatter plot of the data. The data appear to lie on a _____ .

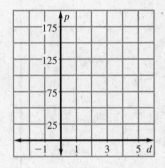

Test whether an exponential model fits the data by finding the ratios of consecutive populations.

$$\frac{\text{Population on Day 1}}{\text{Population on Day 0}} = \frac{}{\underline{\quad}} = \underline{\quad}$$

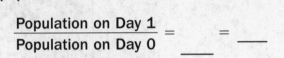

$$\frac{\text{Population on Day 2}}{\text{Population on Day 1}} = \frac{}{\underline{\quad}} = \underline{\quad}$$

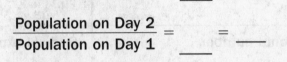

$$\frac{\text{Population on Day 3}}{\text{Population on Day 2}} = \frac{}{\underline{\quad}} = \underline{\quad}$$

The ratios show that each day the population is ____ , or ____ %, larger than the previous day's population. Assuming this pattern applies to all data points, it is appropriate to use the exponential growth model $p = C(1 + r)^d$. The growth rate is ____ and the initial population is ____ .

Check the values of *d* in the exponential model
$p = \underline{\quad}(1 + \underline{\quad})^d$.

When *d* = 3:   **When *d* = 4:**

$p = \underline{\quad}(1 + \underline{\quad})^d$ $p = \underline{\quad}(1 + \underline{\quad})^d$

$p = \underline{\quad}(\underline{\quad})—$ $p = \underline{\quad}(\underline{\quad})—$

$p = \underline{\quad}$ $p = \underline{\quad}$

The exponential model $p = \underline{\quad}(\underline{\quad})^d$ ____ the data.

Words to Review

Give an example of the vocabulary word.

Square root	Positive square root, Negative square root
Radicand	Perfect square
Irrational number	Radical expression
Quadratic equation in standard form	Leading coefficient
Simplest form of a radical expression	Quadratic function in standard form

Vertex	Axis of symmetry
Roots	**Quadratic formula**
Discriminant	**Quadratic inequality**
Parabola	**Graph of a quadratic inequality**

Review your notes and Chapter 9 by using the Chapter Review on pages 562–564 of your textbook.

10.1 Adding and Subtracting Polynomials

Goals • Add and subtract polynomials.
• Use polynomials to model real-life situations.

VOCABULARY

Polynomial

Standard form

Degree

Degree of a polynomial

Leading coefficient

Monomial
Binomial
Trinomial

Example 1 *Identifying Polynomial Coefficients*

Identify the coefficients of $x + 3x^4 - 11x^3 - 9$.

Solution

First write the polynomial in standard form. Account for each de
even if you must use a zero coefficient.

> The coefficient of the *x*-term is 1 because $1 \cdot x = x$.

$x + 3x^4 - 11x^3 - 9 = $ _____

Answer The coefficients are _____.

Example 2 · Classifying Polynomials

Polynomial	Degree	Classified by Degree	Classified by Number of Terms
a. -3	___	_____	_____
b. $-x + 1$	___	_____	_____
c. $x^2 + 3$	___	_____	_____
d. $5x^3 - 3x^2 + x - 8$	___	_____	_____
e. $-x^4 + 2x^3 + 3$	___	_____	_____

Example 3 · Adding Polynomials

To add or subtract two polynomials, add or subtract the like terms. You can use a vertical format or a horizontal format.

Find the sum. Write the answer in standard form.

$(-3x^3 + 11x^2 - 8x + x^5 + 2) + (8x - 2x^4 + 7x^3 - 3 + 12x^2)$

Solution

Write each expression in standard form. Align like terms.

$$x^5 \qquad - 3x^3 + 11x^2 - 8x + 2$$
$$-2x^4 + 7x^3 + 12x^2 + 8x - 3$$

Example 4 · Subtracting Polynomials

Find the difference.

$(11x^4 + x^3 - x + 5) - (-x^4 - x^2 + 2x + 8)$

When subtracting one polynomial from another, don't forget to distribute the subtraction sign to each term of the polynomial that's being subtracted.

Solution

$$11x^4 + x^3 - \ x + 5$$
$$-(-x^4 - x^2 + 2x + 8)$$

Add the opposite.

$$11x^4 + x^3 \qquad - \ x + 5$$
$$\boxed{}x^4 \quad \boxed{}x^2 \ \boxed{}2x \ \boxed{}8$$

✓ *Checkpoint* **Find the sum or difference.**

1. $(2x^6 - x^5 + 3x^3 - 14x^2 + 13) + (7x^5 - x^4 + 9x^3 + 13x^2 + 2)$

2. $(-x^3 - 5x^2 + x - 1) - (-x^3 + 3x^2 + 10x - 9)$

Example 5 *Adding Polynomials*

Population The resident populations, in thousands, of California and Nevada from 1995 through 2001 can be modeled by the following equations, where x is the number of years since 1990.

CA: $C = 4.8106x^4 - 155.662x^3 + 1855.45x^2 - 9171.3x + 47,6$

NV: $N = 0.8826x^4 - 27.659x^3 + 315.64x^2 - 1465.3x + 3924$

Find a model for the resident population P of California and Neva combined for 1995 through 2001.

Solution

You can find a model P by adding the models C and N.

$$4.8106x^4 - 155.662x^3 + 1855.45x^2 - 9171.3x + 47,623$$
$$+\ 0.8826x^4 - 27.659x^3 + 315.64x^2 - 1465.3x + 3924$$

Answer The model for the resident population P of California and Nevada combined for 1995 through 2001 is

$P =$ _____

10.2 Multiplying Polynomials

Goals • Multiply two polynomials.
• Use polynomial multiplication in real-life situations.

VOCABULARY

FOIL

Example 1 *Using the Distributive Property*

Find the product $(x - 5)(x + 7)$.

$(x - 5)(x + 7) = \underline{\quad}(x + 7) - \underline{\quad}(x + 7)$ $(b - c)a = ba - ca$

$= \underline{\hspace{3cm}}$ $a(b + c) = ab + ac$

$= \underline{\hspace{2cm}}$ **Combine like terms.**

Example 2 *Multiplying Binomials Using the FOIL Pattern*

$$\overset{\text{F}}{\downarrow} \quad \overset{\text{O}}{\downarrow} \quad \overset{\text{I}}{\downarrow} \quad \overset{\text{L}}{\downarrow}$$

$(x - 5)(7x + 1) = \underline{\hspace{4cm}}$

$= \underline{\hspace{3cm}}$

Example 3 *Multiplying Polynomials Vertically*

Find the product $(4 - x)(8 - 11x + x^2)$.

Align like terms in columns.

> To multiply
> o polynomials,
> member that *each*
> m of one
> ynomial must be
> ltiplied by each
> m of the other
> lynomial.

$\times$ _____

_____

Standard form

Standard form

$8(-x + 4)$

$-11x(-x + 4)$

$x^2(-x + 4)$

Combine like terms.

Example 4   *Multiplying Polynomials Horizontally*

Find the product $(2x^3 - 9x^2 - 11x)(2 - x^2)$.

Solution Multiply $2 - x^2$ by each term of $2x^3 - 9x^2 - 11x$.

> Remember to use the product of powers property when multiplying two variable terms.

$(2x^3 - 9x^2 - 11x)(2 - x^2)$

$= \underline{\quad}(2 - x^2) - \underline{\quad}(2 - x^2) - \underline{\quad}(2 - x^2)$

$= \underline{\hspace{6cm}}$

$= \underline{\hspace{6cm}}$

Example 5   *Multiplying Binomials to Find an Area*

The diagram at the right shows the basic dimensions for a swimming pool. The pool has a length-to-width ratio of 5 : 2. The walkway measures 2 meters on each side of the width and 3 meters on each side of the length.

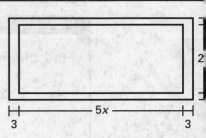

a. Write a polynomial expression that represents the total area of the swimming pool, including the walkway.

b. Find the area when $x = 10, 20, 30, 40,$ and 50 meters.

Solution

a. Use a verbal model.

PROBLEM SOLVING STRATEGY

Verbal Model | Total area | = | | • | |

Labels   Total area = $\underline{\quad}$ (square mete

        Length of pool and walkway = $\underline{\hspace{2cm}}$ (meters)

        Width of pool and walkway = $\underline{\hspace{2cm}}$ (meters)

Algebraic Model $A = \underline{\hspace{4cm}}$ Area model

        $= \underline{\hspace{4cm}}$ FOIL pattern

        $= \underline{\hspace{4cm}}$ Combine like term

b. Evaluate the polynomial expression by substituting x-values.

x(m)	10	20	30	40	50
A(m^2)					

✔ Checkpoint Write your answers in standard form.

1. Find the product $(13 - x^2)(x + 2)$.

---

2. Find the product $(11x^2 + 7x - 3)(-5x + 1)$.

---

3. A picture has a length-to-width ratio of $3:2$. The frame adds 1 inch to each side.

   a. Sketch and label the picture and frame.

   b. Write a polynomial expression that represents the total area A of the picture, including the frame.

   c. Find the area when $x = 2, 3, 4$, and 5 inches.

10.3 Special Products of Polynomials

Goals • Use special product patterns for the product of a sum and difference, and for the square of a binomial.
• Use special products as real-life models.

SPECIAL PRODUCT PATTERNS

Sum and Difference Pattern

$(a + b)(a - b) = a^2 - b^2$ **Example:** $(3x - 4)(3x + 4) = $ _____

Square of a Binomial Pattern

$(a + b)^2 = a^2 + 2ab + b^2$ **Example:** $(x + 4)^2 = $ _____

$(a - b)^2 = a^2 - 2ab + b^2$ **Example:** $(2x - 6)^2 = $ _____

Example 1   *Using the Sum and Difference Pattern*

Find the product $(9w + 3)(9w - 3)$.

Solution

$(a + b)(a - b) = $ _____   **Write pattern.**

$(9w + 3)(9w - 3) = $ _____   **Apply pattern.**

$= $ _____   **Simplify.**

> You can use the FOIL pattern to check your answer.

Example 2   *Squaring a Binomial*

Find the product.

a. $(12x + 4)^2$ **b.** $(3k - 2m)^2$

Solution

a. $(a + b)^2 = $ _____   **Write pattern.**

$(12x + 4)^2 = $ _____   **Apply pattern.**

$= $ _____   **Simplify.**

b. $(a - b)^2 = $ _____   **Write pattern.**

$(3k - 2m)^2 = $ _____   **Apply pattern.**

$= $ _____   **Simplify.**

Example 3 *Special Products and Mental Math*

Use mental math to find the product.

a. $47 \cdot 53$ **b.** 63^2

Solution

a. $47 \cdot 53 = $ _____   Write as product of difference and sum.

  $= $ _____   Apply pattern.

  $= $ _____   Simplify.

b. $63^2 = $ _____   Write as square of binomial.

  $= $ _____   Apply pattern.

  $= $ _____   Simplify.

Example 4 *Finding an Area*

Geometry Connection Find an expression for the area A of the shaded region.

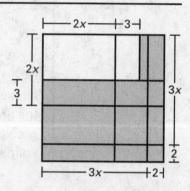

Solution

PROBLEM SOLVING STRATEGY

Verbal Model | Area of shaded region | = | | − | |

Labels   Area of shaded region = ___   (square units)

  Area of entire square = _____   (square units)

  Area of white region = _____   (square units)

Algebraic Model $A = $ _____   Write algebraic model.

  $= $ _____   Apply patterns.

  $= $ _____   Use distributive property.

  $= $ _____   Simplify.

Example 5 *Modeling a Punnett Square*

	G	g
G	GG (green)	Gg (green)
g	Gg (green)	gg (yellow)

Science Connection The Punnett square at the right is an area model that shows the possible results of crossing two pea plants that are each heterogeneous for pod color, carrying the dominant green-pod allele G and the recessive yellow-pod allele g. Each parent pea plant passes along only one allele for color to its offspring.

> A homogeneous gene has two alleles of the same type. A heterogeneous gene has two alleles, one dominant and one recessive.

> Each gene is comprised of two alleles, exactly one of which will be passed on to the offspring from each parent.

Show how the square of a binomial can be used to model the Punnett square.

Solution

Each parent pea plant's pod color genes have a green-pod allele and a yellow-pod allele, so you can model the genetic makeup of each parent as ____G + ____g. The genetic makeup of the offspring can be modeled by the product $($____$G +$ ____$g)^2$.

$$(\underline{\quad}G + \underline{\quad}g)^2 = (\underline{\quad\quad})^2 + 2(\underline{\quad\quad})(\underline{\quad\quad}) + (\underline{\quad\quad})^2$$
$$= \underline{\quad\quad} + \underline{\quad\quad} + \underline{\quad\quad}$$

Answer Theoretically, ____% of the offspring will be homogeneous for green pods, ____% will have green pods but will also carry the recessive yellow-pod allele, and ____% will be homogeneous for yellow pods.

1. Find the product $(11m + 2)(11m - 2)$.	2. Find the product $(9c - 1)^2$.

3. Explain how to use mental math to evaluate the power 99^2.

4. Find an expression for the area of the shaded region.

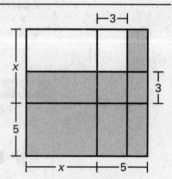

5. Two pea plants are crossed, each heterogeneous for seed shape. Their seed shape genes consist of the dominant round-seed-shape allele and the recessive wrinkled-seed-shape allele. What percent of the offspring will theoretically have wrinkled seeds?

Solving Polynomial Equations in Factored Form

Goals • Solve a polynomial equation in factored form.
• Relate factors and *x*-intercepts.

VOCABULARY

Factored form

Zero-product property

ZERO-PRODUCT PROPERTY

Let *a* and *b* be real numbers. If $ab = 0$, then _____ or _____.

Example 1   *Using the Zero-Product Property*

Solve the equation $(x + 17)(x - 12) = 0$.

Solution Use the zero-product property: either _____ = 0 or _____ = 0.

$(x + 17)(x - 12) = 0$	**Write original equation.**
$x + 17 =$ ___	**Set first factor equal to ___.**
$x =$ _____	**Solve for *x*.**
$x - 12 =$ __	**Set second factor equal to ___.**
$x =$ ___	**Solve for *x*.**

Answer The solutions are $x =$ _____ and $x =$ ___. Check these in the original equation.

Example 2 *Solving a Repeated-Factor Equation*

> This equation
> as a *repeated*
> factor. To solve the
> equation you need
> to set only $x - 9$
> equal to zero.

$$(x - 9)^2 = 0 \qquad \text{Original equation}$$

$$\underline{\hspace{2cm}} = 0 \qquad \text{Set repeated factor equal to 0.}$$

$$x = \underline{\hspace{1cm}} \qquad \text{Solve for } x.$$

Example 3 *Solving a Factored Cubic Equation*

Solve $(7x + 3)(2x - 1)(x + 5) = 0$.

Solution

$$(7x + 3)(2x - 1)(x + 5) = 0 \qquad \text{Write original equation.}$$

$$7x + 3 = \underline{\hspace{0.5cm}} \qquad \text{Set first factor equal to } \underline{\hspace{0.5cm}}.$$

$$x = \underline{\hspace{1cm}} \qquad \text{Solve for } x.$$

> A polynomial
> equation in one
> variable can have as
> many solutions as it
> has linear factors
> that include the
> variable. As you saw
> in Example 2, an
> equation may have
> fewer solutions than
> factors if a factor is
> repeated.

$$2x - 1 = \underline{\hspace{0.5cm}} \qquad \text{Set second factor equal to } \underline{\hspace{0.5cm}}.$$

$$x = \underline{\hspace{1cm}} \qquad \text{Solve for } x.$$

$$x + 5 = \underline{\hspace{0.5cm}} \qquad \text{Set third factor equal to } \underline{\hspace{0.5cm}}.$$

$$x = \underline{\hspace{1cm}} \qquad \text{Solve for } x.$$

Answer The solutions are $\underline{\hspace{1cm}}$, $\underline{\hspace{0.5cm}}$, and $\underline{\hspace{1cm}}$. Check these in the original equation.

✔ *Checkpoint* **Solve the equation.**

1. $(3x - 7)(x + 2)(4x + 9) = 0$

2. $(x + 1)^2 = 0$

FACTORS, SOLUTIONS, AND X-INTERCEPTS

For any quadratic polynomial $ax^2 + bx + c$, if one of the following statements is true, then all three statements are true.

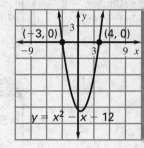

- $(x - p)$ is a factor of the quadratic expression $ax^2 + bx + c$.
  Example: $(x - 4)$ and $(x + 3)$ are factors of $x^2 - x - 12$.

- $x = p$ is a solution of the quadratic equation $ax^2 + bx + c = 0$.
  Example: $x = $ ___ and $x = $ ____ are solutions of $x^2 - x - 12 = 0$.

- p is an x-intercept of the graph of the function $y = ax^2 + bx + c$.
  Example: ___ and ____ are x-intercepts of $y = x^2 - x - 12$.

Example 4 *Relating x-Intercepts and Factors*

To sketch the graph of $y = (x - 3)(x + 7)$:

First solve $(x - 3)(x + 7) = 0$ to find the x-intercepts: ___ and ____.

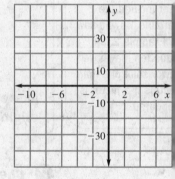

Then find the coordinates of the vertex.

- The x-coordinate of the vertex is the average of the x-intercepts.

  $x = $ _____

- Substitute to find the y-coordinate.

  $y = $ _____

Sketch the graph by using x-intercepts and vertex cooordinates.

- The coordinates of the vertex are (____ , _____).

Example 5   *Using a Quadratic Model*

An opening to a cave can be modeled by the equation

$y = -\dfrac{5}{9}(x + 3)(x - 3)$, with x and y

measured in feet. How wide is the opening at the base? How high is the opening?

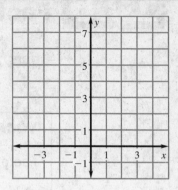

Solution Sketch a graph of the model.

- The x-intercepts are ____ and __.

- The vertex is at _____.

Answer The opening is __ feet wide at the base and __ feet high.

✔ *Checkpoint* **Complete the following exercises.**

---

3. Find the x-intercepts of the function $y = (x + 6)(x + 1)$.

---

4. A tunnel entrance can be modeled by the equation

$y = -\dfrac{5}{16}(x + 8)(x - 8)$, with x and y measured in feet.

How wide is the tunnel at the base? How high is the tunnel?

10.5 Factoring $x^2 + bx + c$

Goals • Factor a quadratic expression of the form $x^2 + bx + c$.
• Solve quadratic equations by factoring.

VOCABULARY

Factor

FACTORING $x^2 + bx + c$

You know from the FOIL method that $(x + p)(x + q) = x^2 + (p + q)x + pq$. So to factor $x^2 + bx + c$, you need to find numbers p and q such that $p + q = b$ and $pq = c$ because $x^2 + (p + q)x + pq = x^2 + bx + c$ if and only if $p + q = b$ and $pq = c$.

Example: $x^2 + 6x + 8 = (x + \underline{})(x + \underline{})$

$\underline{} + \underline{} = 6$ and $\underline{} \cdot \underline{} = 8$

Example 1 *Factoring when c is Positive*

Factor.   **a.** $x^2 + 17x + 60$ **b.** $x^2 - 16x + 39$

Solution

> You can check the result by using the FOIL pattern. When you multiply, you should get the given form of the trinomial.

a. Because b and c are positive, both p and q must be positive. Yo need to find two numbers whose _____ is 17 and whose _____ is 60.

$x^2 + 17x + 60 = (x + p)(x + q)$ **Find p and q when**
                                       _____ = 17 and _____ = 6

$ = (x + \underline{})(x + \underline{})$ $p = \underline{}$ and $q = \underline{}$

b. Because b is negative and c is positive, both p and q must be _____ numbers. Find two numbers whose sum is _____ and whose product is ___.

$x^2 - 16x + 39 = (x + p)(x + q)$ **Find p and q when**
                                       $p + q = $ _____ and
                                       $pq = $ ___.

$ = (x - \underline{})(x - \underline{})$ $p = $ _____ and $q = $ __

Example 2   *Factoring when c is Negative*

Factor.   **a.** $x^2 - 12x - 64$ **b.** $x^2 + 10x - 75$

Solution

a. For this trinomial, b and c are negative. Because c is negative, you know that p and q must have _____.

$$x^2 - 12x - 64 = (x + p)(x + q)$$ Find p and q when
$p + q =$ _____ and
$pq =$ _____.

$= $ _____ $p =$ _____ and $q =$ ___

b. For this trinomial, b is positive and c is negative. Because c is negative, you know that p and q must have _____.

$$x^2 + 10x - 75 = (x + p)(x + q)$$ Find p and q when
$p + q =$ ___ and
$pq =$ _____.

$= $ _____ $p =$ ___ and $q =$ _____

Example 3   *Using the Discriminant*

> A quadratic trinomial $x^2 + bx + c$ can be factored into linear factors with integer coefficients only if the discriminant is a perfect square.

Tell whether the trinomial can be factored into linear factors with integer coefficients.

a. $x^2 - 8x + 12$ **b.** $x^2 + 9x - 1$

Solution Find the discriminant.

a. $b^2 - 4ac = ($___$)^2 - 4($__$)($__$)$ $a =$ __ , $b =$ _____ , $c =$ ___
$=$ ___   **Simplify.**

Answer The discriminant ___ a perfect square, so the trinomial _____ be factored into linear factors with integer coefficients.

b. $b^2 - 4ac = $ _____ $a =$ __ , $b =$ __ , $c =$ ___
$=$ ___   **Simplify.**

Answer The discriminant _____ a perfect square, so the trinomial _____ be factored into linear factors with integer coefficients.

Example 4   Solving a Quadratic Equation

$$x^2 - 6x = 72 \qquad \text{Original equation}$$

$$x^2 - 6x \ \underline{\quad} \ 72 = 0 \qquad \text{Write in standard form.}$$

$$\underline{\hspace{3cm}} = 0 \qquad \text{Factor left side.}$$

$$\underline{\hspace{1.5cm}} = 0 \ \text{or} \ \underline{\hspace{1.5cm}} = 0 \qquad \text{Use zero-product property.}$$

$$\underline{\hspace{1.5cm}} = 0 \qquad \text{Set first factor equal to 0.}$$

$$x = \underline{\quad} \qquad \text{Solve for } x.$$

$$\underline{\hspace{1.5cm}} = 0 \qquad \text{Set second factor equal to 0}$$

$$x = \underline{\quad} \qquad \text{Solve for } x.$$

Answer The solutions are $\underline{\quad}$ and $\underline{\quad}$.

Example 5   Writing a Quadratic Model

You are putting a deck on two sides of a whirlpool that measures 6 feet by 3 feet. You have 10 square feet of wood to make the deck. How wide should the deck be?

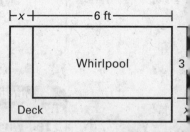

Area of border	=	Total area	−	Whirlpool area

Write a verbal model.

$$\underline{\hspace{6cm}} \qquad \text{Write quadratic model.}$$

$$\underline{\hspace{6cm}} \qquad \text{Multiply.}$$

$$\underline{\hspace{6cm}} \qquad \text{Write in standard form.}$$

$$\underline{\hspace{6cm}} \qquad \text{Factor.}$$

$$\underline{\hspace{6cm}} \qquad \text{Use zero-product property.}$$

$$\underline{\hspace{6cm}} \qquad \text{Solve for } x.$$

Answer Because $x = \underline{\hspace{1.5cm}}$ is not reasonable, the width is $\underline{\quad}$ foot.

 Checkpoint Solve the equation.

1. $x^2 + x - 42 = 0$	**2.** $x^2 - 17x - 18 = 20$

10.6 Factoring $ax^2 + bx + c$

Goals • Factor a quadratic expression of the form $ax^2 + bx + c$.
• Solve quadratic equations by factoring.

Example 1   *One Pair of Factors for a and c*

Factor $3x^2 + 22x + 7$.

Solution Test the possible factors of a (1 and 3) and c (1 and 7).

Try $a = 1 \cdot 3$ and $c = 1 \cdot 7$.

$$(\_x + \_)(\_x + \_) = \_x^2 + \_\_x + \_$$

Now try $a = 1 \cdot 3$ and $c = 7 \cdot 1$.

$$(\_x + \_)(\_x + \_) = \_x^2 + \_\_x + \_$$

Answer The correct factorization is _____.

Example 2   *Several Pairs of Factors for a and c*

Factor $8x^2 - 21x + 10$.

> To factor quadratic trinomials, find the factors of and c so that the um of the outer and nner products is b.

Factors of a and c	Product	Correct?
$a = 1 \cdot \_\_$ and $c = (-1)(\_\_)$	_____ = _____	___
$a = 1 \cdot \_\_$ and $c = (-10)(\_\_)$	_____ = _____	___
$a = 1 \cdot \_\_$ and $c = (-2)(\_\_)$	_____ = _____	___
$a = 1 \cdot \_\_$ and $c = (-5)(\_\_)$	_____ = _____	___
$a = 2 \cdot \_\_$ and $c = (-1)(\_\_)$	_____ = _____	___
$a = 2 \cdot \_\_$ and $c = (-10)(\_\_)$	_____ = _____	___
$a = 2 \cdot \_\_$ and $c = (-2)(\_\_)$	_____ = _____	___
$a = 2 \cdot \_\_$ and $c = (-5)(\_\_)$	_____ = _____	___

Answer The correct factorization is _____.

Example 3 A Common Factor for a, b, and c

Factor $9x^2 + 42x - 15$.

Solution

Begin by factoring out the common factor __.

$$9x^2 + 42x - 15 = \underline{}(\underline{}x^2 + \underline{}x - \underline{})$$

Now factor $\underline{}x^2 + \underline{}x - \underline{}$ by testing the possible factors of a and c.

Factors of a and c	Product	Correc
$a = 1 \cdot \underline{}$ and $c = (-1)(\underline{})$	_____ = _____	___
$a = 1 \cdot \underline{}$ and $c = (5)(\underline{})$	_____ = _____	___
$a = 1 \cdot \underline{}$ and $c = (1)(\underline{})$	_____ = _____	___
$a = 1 \cdot \underline{}$ and $c = (-5)(\underline{})$	_____ = _____	___

Answer The correct factorization is _____.

Example 4 Solving a Quadratic Equation

Solve the equation $28n^2 + 20n + 3 = -34n - 15$.

Solution

$$28n^2 + 20n + 3 = -34n - 15 \qquad \text{Write equation.}$$

$$\underline{} + \underline{} + \underline{} = 0 \qquad \text{Write in standard form.}$$

$$\underline{}(\underline{} + \underline{} + \underline{}) = 0 \qquad \text{Factor out common facto}$$

$$\underline{}(\underline{})(\underline{}) = 0 \qquad \text{Factor trinomial.}$$

$$\underline{} = 0 \text{ or } \underline{} = 0 \qquad \text{Use zero-product proper}$$

$$n = \underline{} \quad \text{or} \quad n = \underline{} \qquad \text{Solve for } n.$$

> Between steps 4 and 5, each side was divided by 2.

Answer The solutions are $\underline{}$ and $\underline{}$.

Example 5 *Writing a Quadratic Model*

A ball is thrown directly upward from a height 100 feet above the ground with an initial speed of 60 feet per second. How long will it take the ball to hit the ground?

Solution Use the equation $s_f = \frac{1}{2}gt^2 + v_i t + s_i$, where s_i is initial position, s_f is final position, g is -32 feet per second squared, v_i is initial velocity, and t is time.

$s_f = \frac{1}{2}gt^2 + v_i t + s_i$	**Vertical motion model**
$0 = \frac{1}{2}(\underline{\quad})t^2 + \underline{\quad}t + \underline{\quad\quad}$	**Substitute values.**
$0 = \underline{\quad\quad}t^2 + \underline{\quad}t + \underline{\quad\quad}$	**Simplify.**
$0 = \underline{\quad\quad\quad\quad\quad\quad}$	**Factor out** $\underline{\quad}$.
$0 = \underline{\quad\quad\quad\quad\quad}$	**Factor.**
$\underline{\quad\quad} = 0$ or $\underline{\quad\quad} = 0$	**Use zero-product property.**
$t = \underline{\quad\quad}$ or $t = \underline{\quad}$	**Solve for t.**

In step 4, factor out a negative common factor to make the leading coefficient positive.

Answer The solutions are $\underline{\quad\quad}$ and $\underline{\quad}$. Negative values for time do not make sense, so the only reasonable solution is $t = \underline{\quad}$. It will take $\underline{\quad}$ seconds for the ball to hit the ground.

✔ *Checkpoint* **Complete the following exercises.**

1. Factor $28x^2 - 5x - 12$.	**2.** Factor $12n^2 - 26n + 12$.

3. Solve $23x^2 - 20x + 17 = -10x^2 + 31x - 1$.

4. A ball is thrown directly upward from an initial position of 200 feet above the ground with an initial speed of 140 feet per second. How long will it take the ball to hit the ground?

10.7 Factoring Special Products

Goals • Use special product patterns to factor quadratic polynomia
• Solve quadratic equations by factoring.

FACTORING SPECIAL PRODUCTS

Difference of Two Squares Pattern	**Example**
$a^2 - b^2 = (a + b)(a - b)$	$9x^2 - 16 = (\underline{\quad} + \underline{\quad})(\underline{\quad} - \underline{\quad}$
Perfect Square Trinomial Pattern	**Example**
$a^2 + 2ab + b^2 = (a + b)^2$	$x^2 + 8x + 16 = (\underline{\quad} + \underline{\quad})^2$
$a^2 - 2ab + b^2 = (a - b)^2$	$x^2 - 12x + 36 = (\underline{\quad} - \underline{\quad})^2$

Example 1 *Factoring the Difference of Two Squares*

a. $n^2 - 225 = \underline{\quad}^2 - \underline{\quad}^2$ Write as $a^2 - b^2$.

$= \underline{\hspace{4cm}}$ Factor using pattern.

b. $121x^2 - 144 = (\underline{\quad})^2 - \underline{\quad}^2$ Write as $a^2 - b^2$.

$= \underline{\hspace{4cm}}$ Factor using pattern.

c. $243p^2 - 147 = \underline{\quad}(\underline{\quad}p^2 - \underline{\quad})$ Factor out common factor

$= \underline{\quad}[(\underline{\quad})^2 - \underline{\quad}^2]$ Write as $a^2 - b^2$.

$= \underline{\hspace{4cm}}$ Factor using pattern.

Example 2 *Factoring Perfect Square Trinomials*

a. $x^2 + 40x + 400$

$= \underline{\quad}^2 + 2(\underline{\quad})(\underline{\quad}) + \underline{\quad}^2$ Write as $a^2 + 2ab + b^2$.

$= (\underline{\hspace{2cm}})^2$ Factor using pattern.

b. $9y^2 - 12y + 4$

$= (\underline{\quad})^2 - 2(\underline{\quad})(\underline{\quad}) + \underline{\quad}^2$ Write as $a^2 - 2ab + b^2$.

$= (\underline{\hspace{2cm}})^2$ Factor using pattern.

c. $5c^2 + 40c + 80$

$= \underline{\quad}(\underline{\quad}^2 + \underline{\quad}c + \underline{\quad})$ Factor out common factor.

$= \underline{\quad}[\underline{\quad}^2 + 2(\underline{\quad})(\underline{\quad}) + \underline{\quad}^2]$ Write as $a^2 + 2ab + b^2$

$= \underline{\quad}(\underline{\hspace{2cm}})^2$ Factor using pattern.

Example 3 *Graphical and Analytical Reasoning*

Solve the equation $9x^2 - 25 = 0$.

Solution

$$9x^2 - 25 = 0$$ Write original equation.

$$\underline{\hspace{3cm}} = 0$$ Write as $a^2 - b^2$.

$$\underline{\hspace{3cm}} = 0$$ Factor using pattern.

$$\underline{\hspace{2cm}} = 0 \text{ or } \underline{\hspace{2cm}} = 0$$ Use zero-product property.

$$x = \underline{\hspace{1.5cm}} \text{ or } x = \underline{\hspace{1.5cm}}$$ Solve for x.

Answer The solutions are $\underline{\hspace{1.5cm}}$ and $\underline{\hspace{1cm}}$.

Check You can check your answer by substitution or by graphing.

Graph $y = 9x^2 - 25$.

Use your graphing calculator's *zero feature* to find the x-intercepts, where $9x^2 - 25 = 0$.

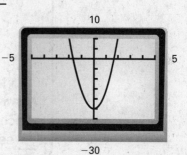

Example 4 *Solving a Quadratic Equation*

Solve $\dfrac{4}{100}x^2 - \dfrac{3}{10}x + \dfrac{9}{16} = 0$.

Solution

$$\dfrac{4}{100}x^2 - \dfrac{3}{10}x + \dfrac{9}{16} = 0$$ Write original equation.

$$\underline{\hspace{1.5cm}} - \underline{\hspace{1.5cm}} + \underline{\hspace{1.5cm}} = 0$$ Write as $a^2 - 2ab + b^2$.

$$\underline{\hspace{3cm}} = 0$$ Factor using pattern.

$$\underline{\hspace{3cm}} = 0$$ Set repeated factor equal to 0.

$$x = \underline{\hspace{1.5cm}}$$ Solve for x.

Answer The solution is $\underline{\hspace{1.5cm}}$. Check this in the original equation.

Example 5 *Using a Quadratic Model*

Vertical Motion An object is propelled from the ground with an initial upward velocity of 128 feet per second. Will the object reach a height of 256 feet? If it does, how long will it take the object to reach the height?

Solution

Use a vertical motion model where v is 128, s is 0, and h is 256.

$-16t^2 + vt + s = h$	**Vertical motion model**
$-16t^2 + \underline{\quad}t + \underline{\,} = \underline{\quad}$	**Substitute for v, s, and h.**
$-16t^2 + \underline{\quad}t - \underline{\quad} = 0$	**Write in standard form.**
$\underline{\hspace{3cm}} = 0$	**Factor out common factor.**
$\underline{\hspace{2.5cm}} = 0$	**Factor.**
$\underline{\hspace{1.5cm}} = 0$	**Set repeated factor equal to**
$t = \underline{\,}$	**Solve for t.**

Answer Because there is a solution, you know that the object will reach a height of 256 feet. The solution is $t = \underline{\,}$, so it will take $\underline{\,}$ seconds to reach that height.

✔ *Checkpoint* **Complete the following exercises.**

1. Factor $\dfrac{16}{25}m^2 - \dfrac{1}{4}$.

2. Solve the equation $-9x^2 + 84x - 196 = 0$.

3. An object is propelled from the ground with an initial upward velocity of 256 feet per second. Will it reach a height of 1024 feet? If it does, how long will it take it to reach the height?

Factoring Using the Distributive Property

Goals • Use the distributive property to factor a polynomial.
• Solve polynomial equations by factoring.

VOCABULARY

Prime _____

_____

Factor a polynomial completely _____

Example 1 *Factoring Completely*

Factor $14x^3 - 77x^2 - 42x$ completely.

Solution First find the greatest common factor.

$14x^3 = $ _____

$77x^2 = $ _____

$42x = $ _____

$GCF = $ _____

Then use the distributive property to factor the greatest common factor out of the polynomial.

$14x^3 - 77x^2 - 42x = $ _____   **Factor out GCF.**

$= $ _____   **Factor $ax^2 + bx + c$.**

Example 2 *Factoring Completely*

Factor $250x^5 - 800x^4 + 640x^3$ completely.

Solution

$250x^5 - 800x^4 + 640x^3$

$= $ _____   **Factor out GCF.**

$= $ _____   **Factor $ax^2 - 2ab + b^2$.**

Example 3 *Factoring by Grouping*

Factor $5x^3 + 2x^2 + 5x + 2$ completely.

$5x^3 + 2x^2 + 5x + 2$

$= (5x^3 + \underline{\quad}) + (\underline{\quad} + 2)$ Group terms.

$= \underline{\quad\quad\quad\quad} + \underline{\quad\quad\quad\quad}$ Factor each group.

$= \underline{\quad\quad\quad\quad\quad}$ Use distributive property.

WAYS TO SOLVE POLYNOMIAL EQUATIONS

Graphing Can be used to solve any equation, but gives only appoximate solutions.

The Quadratic Formula Can be used to solve any *quadratic* equation.

Factoring Can be used with the zero-product property to solve an equation that is factorable.

- **Factoring**

  $x^2 + bx + c$

  $ax^2 + bx + c$

  Example

  $x^2 + 9x + 18 = (\underline{\quad})(\underline{\quad})$

  $3x^2 + 10x + 7 = (\underline{\quad})(\underline{\quad})$

- **Special Products**

  $a^2 - b^2 = (a + b)(a - b)$

  $a^2 + 2ab + b^2 = (a + b)^2$

  $a^2 - 2ab + b^2 = (a - b)^2$

  Example

  $4x^2 - 36 = (\underline{\quad})(\underline{\quad})$

  $x^2 + 18x + 81 = (\underline{\quad})^2$

  $x^2 - 16x + 64 = (\underline{\quad})^2$

- **Factoring Completely**

✔ *Checkpoint* **Factor the polynomial completely.**

1. $12x^4 + 36x^3 + 27x^2$	2. $32x^3 - 16x^2 - 98x + 49$
3. $9x^5 + 270x^4 + 15x^3$	4. $45x^3 + 9x^2 + 5x + 1$

Example 4 **Solving Polynomials**

Solve the equation.

a. $3x^3 + 2x^2 - 3x - 2 = 0$ **b.** $21x^3 + 28x^2 = 14x$

Solution

a. $3x^3 + 2x^2 - 3x - 2 = 0$ Write original equation.

$(\underline{\hspace{1cm}} - 3x) + (2x^2 - \underline{\hspace{0.5cm}}) = 0$ Group terms.

$\underline{\hspace{0.5cm}}(\underline{\hspace{1.5cm}}) + \underline{\hspace{0.5cm}}(\underline{\hspace{1.5cm}}) = 0$ Factor each group.

$(\underline{\hspace{1.5cm}})(\underline{\hspace{1.5cm}}) = 0$ Use distributive property.

$(\underline{\hspace{1cm}})(\underline{\hspace{1cm}})(\underline{\hspace{1cm}}) = 0$ Factor $a^2 - b^2$.

Answer Set each variable factor equal to zero. The solutions are

$\underline{\hspace{1cm}}$, $\underline{\hspace{0.5cm}}$, and $\underline{\hspace{1cm}}$.

> You can also use your graphing calculator's *zero feature* to estimate the *x*-intercepts of a function.

Check Graph $y = 3x^3 + 2x^2 - 3x - 2$.
Use your calculator's TRACE feature to estimate the *x*-intercepts.

The graph appears to confirm the solutions.

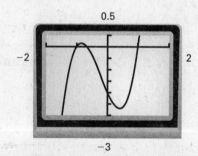

b. $21x^3 + 28x^2 - 14x = 0$ Rewrite equation in standard form.

$\underline{\hspace{0.5cm}}(\underline{\hspace{2.5cm}}) = 0$ Factor out GCF.

Answer $\underline{\hspace{0.5cm}}$ factors out, so one solution is $\underline{\hspace{0.5cm}}$. Because $3x^2 + 4x - 2$ is not factorable, use the quadratic formula to find the other solutions, $x \approx \underline{\hspace{1cm}}$ and $x \approx \underline{\hspace{1cm}}$.

Check Graph $y = 21x^3 + 28x^2 - 14x$.
Use your calculator's TRACE feature to estimate the *x*-intercepts.

The graph appears to confirm the solutions.

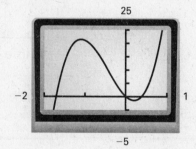

Words to Review

Give an example of the vocabulary word.

Polynomial	Standard form of a polynomial
Degree of a term	Degree of a polynomial
Leading coefficient	Monomial
Binomial	Trinomial
FOIL pattern	Factored form of a polynomial
Zero-product property	Factor a quadratic expression
Prime factor	Factor a polynomial completely

Review your notes and Chapter 10 by using the Chapter Review on pages 634–636 of your textbook.

Ratio and Proportion

Goals • Solve proportions.
• Use proportions to solve real-life problems.

VOCABULARY

Proportion

Extremes

Means

Solving the proportion

Extraneous solution

PROPERTIES OF PROPORTIONS

Reciprocal Property

If two ratios are _____ , their reciprocals, if they exist, are also _____ .

If $\dfrac{a}{b} = \dfrac{c}{d}$, then $\dfrac{b}{a} = \dfrac{d}{c}$.   **Example:** $\dfrac{2}{3} = \dfrac{4}{6}$ ➡ $\dfrac{3}{2} = \dfrac{6}{4}$

Cross Product Property

The product of the _____ equals the product of the _____ .

If $\dfrac{a}{b} = \dfrac{c}{d}$, then $ad = bc$.   **Example:** $\dfrac{2}{3} = \dfrac{4}{6}$ ➡ $2 \cdot 6 = 3 \cdot 4$

Example 1   *Using the Reciprocal Property*

Solve the proportion $\dfrac{4}{y} = \dfrac{3}{7}$.

Solution

$$\dfrac{4}{y} = \dfrac{3}{7}$$ Write original proportion.

$$\dfrac{}{} = \dfrac{}{}$$ Use reciprocal property.

$$y = \dfrac{}{}$$ Multiply each side by ___ .

$$y = \dfrac{}{}$$ Simplify.

Check When you substitute to check, $\boxed{}$ becomes $4 \cdot \dfrac{4}{}$ whic

simplifies to $\dfrac{}{}$.

Example 2   *Using the Cross Product Property*

Solve the proportion $\dfrac{x}{16} = \dfrac{4}{x}$.

Solution

$$\dfrac{x}{16} = \dfrac{4}{x}$$ Write original proportion.

$$x \cdot \underline{} = \underline{} \cdot \underline{}$$ Use cross product property. $\dfrac{x}{16} \Large\diagdown\!\!\!\!\diagup$

$$x^{\boxed{}} = \underline{}$$ Simplify.

$$x = \underline{}$$ Take square root of each side.

Answer The solutions are $x =$ ___ and $x =$ _____ . Check these in th
original proportion.

> Remember to check your solution in the original proportion. Notice that Example 2 has two solutions so you need to check both of them.

Example 3   *Checking Solutions*

When you solve the proportion $\dfrac{x^2 - 16}{x + 4} = \dfrac{x - 4}{3}$, you get two

possible solutions: $x = 4$ and $x = -4$. Check these by substituting in the original proportion.

Solution

Check each solution by substituting it into the original proportion.

$x = \underline{\quad}$:

$$\dfrac{x^2 - 16}{x + 4} = \dfrac{x - 4}{3}$$

$$\dfrac{\boxed{}^2 - 16}{\boxed{} + 4} \overset{?}{=} \dfrac{\boxed{} - 4}{3}$$

$$\underline{\quad} \overset{?}{=} \underline{\quad}$$

$$\underline{\quad}$$

$x = \underline{\quad}$:

$$\dfrac{x^2 - 16}{x + 4} = \dfrac{x - 4}{3}$$

$$\dfrac{(\boxed{})^2 - 16}{(\boxed{}) + 4} \overset{?}{=} \dfrac{(\boxed{}) - 4}{3}$$

$$\underline{\quad}$$

Answer You can conclude that $x = \underline{\quad}$ is extraneous because the check results in a $\underline{\quad}$ statement. The only solution is $x = \underline{\quad}$.

✔ *Checkpoint* **Solve the proportion. Check for extraneous solutions.**

1. $\dfrac{5}{y} = \dfrac{4}{9}$	2. $\dfrac{3}{8} = \dfrac{2}{x}$	3. $\dfrac{4}{7} = \dfrac{2u}{5}$
4. $\dfrac{v + 2}{4} = \dfrac{v}{3}$	5. $\dfrac{3}{y} = \dfrac{2y + 1}{5}$	6. $\dfrac{m}{4m} = \dfrac{2m - 1}{3}$

11.2 Percents

Goals • Use equations to solve percent problems.
• Use percents in real-life applications.

VOCABULARY

Base number

Example 1   *Number Compared to Base is Unknown*

What is 40% of 90 inches?

Solution

Verbal Model $\boxed{a}$ is $\boxed{p\ \text{percent}}$ of $\boxed{b}$

Labels   Number compared to base $= a$ (inches)

Percent $= 40\% = $ ____   (no units)

Base number $= $ ____   (inches)

Algebraic Model $a = ($ ____ $)($ ____ $)$

$= $ ____

Answer ____ inches is 40% of 90 inches.

Example 2 **Base Number is Unknown**

Twelve dollars is 15% of what amount of money?

Solution

Verbal Model $\boxed{a}$ is $\boxed{p \text{ percent}}$ of $\boxed{b}$

     Labels   Number compared to base = ____   (dollars)

                    Percent = 15% = _____   (no units)

                    Base number = b (dollars)

Algebraic Model $\_\_\_ = (\ \_\_\_\_\_\ )b$

                    $\dfrac{}{\_\_\_\_\_} = b$

                    $\_\_\_ = b$

Answer $12 is 15% of $___ .

Example 3 **Percent is Unknown**

Two hundred fifty-five is what percent of 85?

Solution

Verbal Model $\boxed{a}$ is $\boxed{p \text{ percent}}$ of $\boxed{b}$

     Labels   Number compared to base = _____   (no units)

                    Percent = p (no units)

                    Base number = ___   (no units)

Algebraic Model $\_\_\_\_ = p(\ \_\_\_\ )$

                    $\dfrac{}{\_\_\_\_\_} = p$

                    $\_\_\_ = p$ **Decimal form**

                    $\_\_\_\_\_ \% = p$ **Percent form**

Example 4 Modeling and Using Percents

Trees A logging company determined that there are about 180 oak trees on an 8-acre lot. Oak trees make up about 16% of all trees on the lot. Estimate how many trees are on the 8 acres.

Solution

Verbal Model

Number of oak trees	is	p percent	of	Total number of trees

Labels

Number of oak trees = _____   (trees)

Percent = 16% = _____   (no units)

Base number = b (trees)

Algebraic Model

_____ = (_____)b

$$\frac{}{} = b$$

_____ = b

Answer There are about _____ trees on the lot.

Example 5 Using a Proportion

Use a proportion to solve the problem in Example 4.

Write ratios that compare the part to the whole. Let b represent t total number of trees on the lot.

$$\frac{\text{Number of oak trees}}{\text{Total number of trees}} = \frac{16}{100}$$ Write proportion.

$$\frac{\boxed{}}{b} = \frac{16}{100}$$ Substitute.

_____ = _____ · _____   Use cross products.

$$b = \frac{}{}$$ Divide each side by ___

= _____   Simplify.

Answer There are about _____ trees on the lot.

✔ **Checkpoint** Solve the percent problem.

1. What is 65% of $220?	2. 46.5 is 30% of what number?
3. One hundred ninety-six is what percent of 140?	4. Women make up 45% of the students at a college. If there are 2160 female students, how many total students are there?

Direct and Inverse Variation

> Goals • Use direct and inverse variation.
> • Use direct and inverse variations to model real-life situation

---

VOCABULARY

Inverse variation

Constant of variation

MODELS FOR DIRECT AND INVERSE VARIATION

**Direct
Variation**
The variables x and y vary *directly* if for a constant k

$$\frac{y}{x} = k, \text{ or } y = kx, k \neq 0.$$

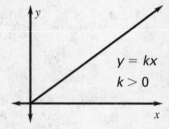

$y = kx$
$k > 0$

**Inverse
Variation**
The variables x and y vary *inversely* if for a constant k

$$xy = k, \text{ or } y = \frac{k}{x}, k \neq 0.$$

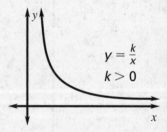

$y = \frac{k}{x}$
$k > 0$

The number k is the constant of variation.

Example 1 *Using Direct and Inverse Variation*

When x is 2, y is 6. Find an equation that relates x and y in each case.

a. x and y vary directly

b. x and y vary inversely

Solution

a. $\dfrac{y}{x} = k$ Write direct variation model.

$\dfrac{}{} = k$ Substitute for x and y.

$\underline{} = k$ Simplify.

Answer The direct variation that relates x and y is $\dfrac{y}{x} = \underline{}$, or $y = \underline{}$.

b. $xy = k$ Write inverse variation model.

$\underline{} = k$ Substitute for x and y.

$\underline{} = k$ Simplify.

Answer The inverse variation that relates x and y is $xy = \underline{}$,

or $y = \dfrac{}{\underline{}}$.

✔ *Checkpoint* The variables x and y vary directly. Use the given values to write an equation that relates x and y.

1. $x = 2$, $y = 10$	**2.** $x = 24$, $y = 6$	**3.** $x = 15$, $y = 35$

4. $x = 4, y = 2$	**5.** $x = 1.5, y = 30$	**6.** $x = 6, y = \dfrac{3}{4}$

Example 2   *Comparing Direct and Inverse Variation*

Compare the direct variation model and the inverse variation mo▮ you found in Example 1 using $x = 1, 2, 3,$ and 4.

a. numerically   **b.** graphically

Solution

a. Use the models $y = 3x$ and $y = \dfrac{12}{x}$ to make a table.

Direct Variation Because *k* is
_____ , *y* _____ as *x*
increases. As *x* increases by 1, *y*
_____ by ___ .

Inverse Variation Because *k* is
_____ , *y* _____ as *x*
increases. As *x* doubles (from 1 to 2),
y is _____ (from 12 to ___).

x-value	1	2	3
Direct, $y = 3x$			
Inverse, $y = \dfrac{12}{x}$			

b. Use the table of values. Plot the points and then connect the points with a smooth curve.

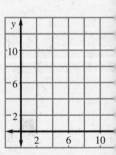

Direct Variation The graph for this model is
a _____ passing through the _____ .

Inverse Variation The graph for this model is
a curve that approaches the _____ as *x*
increases and approaches the *y*-axis as *x*

_____ .

Simplifying Rational Expressions

Goals • Simplify a rational expression.
• Use rational expressions to find geometric probability.

VOCABULARY

Rational number

Rational expression

Simplified rational expression

SIMPLIFYING FRACTIONS

Let a, b, and c be nonzero numbers.

$$\frac{ac}{bc} = \frac{a \cdot \cancel{c}}{b \cdot \cancel{c}} = \frac{a}{b}$$

Example: $\dfrac{28}{35} = \dfrac{4 \cdot \cancel{7}}{5 \cdot \cancel{7}} = \dfrac{4}{5}$

Example 1 — *Factoring Numerator and Denominator*

$$\frac{6x^3}{3x - 12x^2} = \frac{2 \cdot \boxed{}}{\boxed{}(1 - 4x)}$$

Factor numerator and denominator.

$$= \frac{\boxed{}(2\boxed{})}{\boxed{}(1 - 4x)}$$

Divide out common factor ___.

$$= \frac{2\boxed{}}{1 - 4x}$$

Simplified form

Example 2   *Recognizing Opposite Factors*

$$\frac{9 - x^2}{x^2 - 4x + 3} = \frac{(\boxed{})(3 + x)}{(x - 3)(\boxed{})}$$

Factor numerator and denominator.

$$= \frac{-(\boxed{})(x + 3)}{(x - 3)(\boxed{})}$$

Factor -1 from (_____).

$$= -\frac{x + 3}{\boxed{}}$$

Divide out common factor ____ and write simplified form.

✔ *Checkpoint* **Simplify the expression if possible.**

1. $\dfrac{4x(x + 7)}{8x^2}$

2. $\dfrac{3(5 - x)}{12(x - 5)}$

GEOMETRIC PROBABILITY

Region *B* is contained in Region *A*. An object tossed onto Region *A* is equally likely to land on any point in the region.

The geometric probability that the object lands in Region *B* is

$$P = \frac{\text{Area of Region } B}{\text{Area of Region } A}.$$

Example 3 *Writing and Using a Rational Model*

A coin is tossed onto the large rectangular region shown at the right. It is equally likely to land on any point in the region.

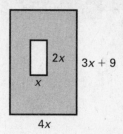

a. Write a model that gives the probability that the coin will land in the small rectangle.

b. Evaluate the model when $x = 4$.

Solution

a. $P = \dfrac{\text{Area of } \boxed{} \text{ rectangle}}{\text{Area of } \boxed{} \text{ rectangle}}$ **Formula for geometric probability**

$= \dfrac{x(\boxed{})}{4x(\boxed{})}$ **Find areas.**

$= \underline{}$ **Divide out common factors.**

$= \underline{}$ **Simplified form**

b. To find the probability when $x = 4$, substitute 4 for x in the model.

$P = \dfrac{x}{6(\boxed{})} = \dfrac{\boxed{}}{6(\boxed{})} = \underline{}$

Answer The probability of landing in the small rectangle is $\underline{}$.

✓ **Checkpoint** Refer to Example 3.

3. Find the probability when $x = 5$.

11.5 Multiplying and Dividing Rational Expressions

Goals • Multiply and divide rational expressions.
• Use rational expressions as real-life models.

MULTIPLYING AND DIVIDING RATIONAL EXPRESSIONS

Let a, b, c, and d be nonzero polynomials.

To multiply, multiply the numerators and the denominators.

$$\frac{a}{b} \cdot \frac{c}{d} = \frac{ac}{bd} \qquad\qquad \text{Example: } \frac{2}{3} \cdot \frac{5}{7} = \frac{10}{21}$$

To divide, multiply by the reciprocal of the divisor.

$$\frac{a}{b} \div \frac{c}{d} = \frac{a}{b} \cdot \frac{d}{c} \qquad\qquad \text{Example: } \frac{2}{3} \div \frac{5}{7} = \frac{2}{3} \cdot \frac{7}{5}$$

Example 1   *Multiplying Rational Expressions Involving Monomials*

Simplify $\dfrac{2x^3}{5x^5} \cdot \dfrac{15x^4}{8x^2}$.

Solution

> When multiplying, you usually factor as far as possible to identify all common factors. For example, you do not need to write the prime factorizations of 24 and 60 in $\dfrac{24}{60}$ if you recognize 12 as their greatest common factor.

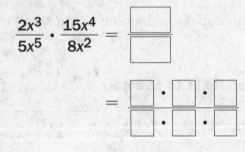

$\dfrac{2x^3}{5x^5} \cdot \dfrac{15x^4}{8x^2} = \dfrac{\boxed{}}{\boxed{}}$ **Multiply numerators and denominators.**

$= \dfrac{\boxed{\ } \cdot \boxed{\ } \cdot \boxed{\ }}{\boxed{\ } \cdot \boxed{\ } \cdot \boxed{\ }}$ **Factor, and divide out common factors.**

$= \underline{}$ **Simplified form**

Example 2 **Multiplying Rational Expressions Involving Polynomials**

$$\frac{3x}{2x^2 - 4x} \cdot \frac{x - 2}{3x^2 + 5x - 2}$$

> When you multiply the numerators and the denominators, leave the products in factored form. At the very end, you may multiply the remaining factors or leave your answer in factored form, as in Example 2.

$$= \frac{3x(x - 2)}{(2x^2 - 4x)(3x^2 + 5x - 2)}$$ Multiply numerators and denominators.

$$= \underline{\hspace{3cm}}$$ Factor, and divide out common factors.

$$= \underline{\hspace{3cm}}$$ Simplified form

Example 3 **Multiplying by a Polynomial**

$$\frac{8x}{x^2 - 7x + 12} \cdot (x - 3)$$

$$= \frac{8x}{x^2 - 7x + 12} \cdot \underline{\hspace{1cm}}$$ Write $x - 3$ as $\underline{\hspace{1.5cm}}$.

$$= \underline{\hspace{2cm}}$$ Multiply numerators and denominators.

$$= \underline{\hspace{2cm}}$$ Factor, and divide out common factors.

$$= \underline{\hspace{1cm}}$$ Simplified form

Example 4 **Dividing Rational Expressions**

$$\frac{n + 7}{4n} \div \frac{n + 7}{n - 2} = \frac{n + 7}{4n} \cdot \underline{\hspace{1.5cm}}$$ Multiply by reciprocal.

$$= \underline{\hspace{3cm}}$$ Multiply numerators and denominators, and divide out common factors.

$$= \underline{\hspace{1.5cm}}$$ Simplified form

Example 5 *Dividing by a Polynomial*

$$\frac{x^2 - 36}{4x^2} \div (x - 6) = \frac{x^2 - 36}{4x^2} \cdot \underline{\hspace{2cm}}$$ Multiply by reciprocal.

$$= \underline{\hspace{3cm}}$$ Multiply numerators and denominators.

$$= \underline{\hspace{3cm}}$$ Factor, and divide out common factors.

$$= \underline{\hspace{1.5cm}}$$ Simplified form

✔ *Checkpoint* **Simplify the expression.**

1. $\dfrac{3y^2}{4y^3} \cdot \dfrac{16y^4}{9y^5}$	2. $\dfrac{4m^2}{3m^2 + 9m} \cdot \dfrac{m + 3}{2m^2 + 3m - 2}$
3. $\dfrac{2n + 3}{n} \div \dfrac{2n + 3}{n + 3}$	4. $\dfrac{x^2 - 25}{2x^3} \div (x + 5)$

11.6 Adding and Subtracting Rational Expressions

Goals
- Add and subtract rational expressions that have like denominators.
- Add and subtract rational expressions that have unlike denominators.

VOCABULARY

Least common denominator (LCD)

ADDING OR SUBTRACTING WITH LIKE DENOMINATORS

Let a, b, and c be polynomials, with $c \neq 0$.

To add, add the numerators.

$$\frac{a}{c} + \frac{b}{c} = \frac{a + b}{c}$$

To subtract, subtract the numerators.

$$\frac{a}{c} - \frac{b}{c} = \frac{a - b}{c}$$

Example 1 *Adding and Subtracting Expressions*

a. $\dfrac{7}{2x} + \dfrac{2x - 7}{2x} = \dfrac{\boxed{} + (\boxed{})}{2x}$ **Add numerators.**

$= \dfrac{}{}$ **Simplify.**

$= \underline{}$ **Simplify.**

b. $\dfrac{5}{3m - 4} - \dfrac{2m}{3m - 4} = \underline{}$ **Subtract numerators.**

✔ Checkpoint Simplify the expression.

1. $\dfrac{5}{3x} + \dfrac{x-6}{3x}$	2. $\dfrac{9}{2n-1} - \dfrac{4n}{2n-1}$

Example 2 *Simplifying After Subtracting*

$$\dfrac{3x}{2x^2 + 3x - 2} - \dfrac{x+1}{2x^2 + 3x - 2}$$

$$= \dfrac{\boxed{} - (\boxed{})}{2x^2 + 3x - 2} \qquad \text{Subtract.}$$

$$= \underline{\hspace{3cm}} \qquad \text{Simplify.}$$

$$= \underline{\hspace{3cm}} \qquad \text{Factor and divide out common factors.}$$

$$= \underline{\hspace{2cm}} \qquad \text{Simplified form}$$

Example 3 *Adding with Unlike Denominators*

Simplify $\dfrac{3}{4x} + \dfrac{1}{6x^2}$.

> You can always find a common denominator by multiplying the two denominators, but it is often easier to use the LCD.

To find the least common denominator, first completely factor the denominators. You get $4x = \underline{} \cdot \underline{}$ and $6x^2 = \underline{} \cdot \underline{} \cdot \underline{}$. The LCD contains the highest power of each factor that appears in either denominator, so the LCD is $\underline{} \cdot \underline{} \cdot \underline{}$, or $\underline{}$.

$$\dfrac{3}{4x} + \dfrac{1}{6x^2} = \dfrac{3 \cdot \boxed{}}{4x \cdot \boxed{}} + \dfrac{1 \cdot \boxed{}}{6x^2 \cdot \boxed{}} \qquad \text{Rewrite fractions using LCD}$$

$$= \dfrac{}{\underline{\hspace{2cm}}} + \dfrac{}{\underline{\hspace{2cm}}} \qquad \text{Simplify numerators and denominators.}$$

$$= \dfrac{}{\underline{\hspace{2cm}}} \qquad \text{Add fractions.}$$

Example 4 **Subtracting with Unlike Denominators**

Simplify $\dfrac{x+3}{x-2} - \dfrac{8}{x+2}$.

Solution Neither denominator can be factored. The least common denominator is the product (_____)(_____) because it must contain both of these factors.

$$\dfrac{x+3}{x-2} - \dfrac{8}{x+2}$$

$$= \dfrac{(x+3)(\boxed{})}{(x-2)(\boxed{})} - \dfrac{8(\boxed{})}{(\boxed{})(x+2)}$$ Rewrite fractions using LCD.

$$= \dfrac{\rule{2cm}{0.4pt}}{\rule{2cm}{0.4pt}} - \dfrac{\rule{2cm}{0.4pt}}{\rule{2cm}{0.4pt}}$$ Simplify numerators. Leave denominators in factored form.

$$= \dfrac{\rule{3cm}{0.4pt}}{\rule{3cm}{0.4pt}}$$ Subtract fractions.

$$= \dfrac{\rule{3cm}{0.4pt}}{\rule{3cm}{0.4pt}}$$ Use distributive property.

$$= \rule{3cm}{0.4pt}$$ Combine like terms.

✓ **Checkpoint** Simplify the expression.

3. $\dfrac{3}{x+3} + \dfrac{4}{x-3}$	4. $\dfrac{2}{x-1} - \dfrac{1}{x+4}$

Dividing Polynomials

> **Goals** • Divide a polynomial by a monomial or by a binomial factor.
> • Use polynomial long division.

Example 1 *Dividing a Polynomial by a Monomial*

Divide $12x^2 + 15x - 18$ by $3x$.

$$\frac{12x^2 + 15x - 18}{3x} = \frac{12x^2}{\boxed{}} + \frac{15x}{\boxed{}} - \frac{18}{\boxed{}}$$
Divide each term numerator by ___

$$= \underline{} + \underline{} - \underline{}$$
Find common factors.

$$= \underline{} + \underline{} - \underline{}$$
Divide out common factors.

$$= \underline{}$$
Simplified form

Example 2 *The Long Division Algorithm*

Use long division to divide 270 by 20.

$$20\overline{)270}$$

1. Think: $\dfrac{27}{20} \approx$ ___

2. Subtract ___ × 20 from 27.

3. Bring down the 0. Think: $\dfrac{\boxed{}}{20} \approx$ ___

4. Subtract ___ × 20 from ___.

5. Remainder is ___.

Quotient   Remainder

Dividend $\longrightarrow$ $\dfrac{270}{20}$ = $\dfrac{}{}$ + $\dfrac{}{}$ = ___ + ___ = ___
Divisor $\longrightarrow$

Example 3   *Polynomial Long Division*

Divide $x^2 + x - 1$ by $x + 3$.

Solution

$$x + 3 \overline{\smash{)}x^2 + x - 1}$$

$$\underline{ - 1}$$

1. Think: $\dfrac{x^2}{x} =$ ___

2. Subtract ___$(x + 3)$.

3. Bring down -1. Think: $\dfrac{\boxed{}}{x} =$ ___

4. Subtract ___$(x + 3)$.

5. Remainder is ___ .

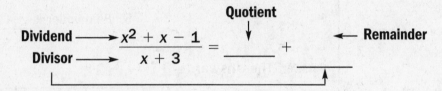

Dividend ⟶ $\dfrac{x^2 + x - 1}{x + 3}$ = Quotient ↓ ___ + ___ ← Remainder

Divisor ⟶

Answer The answer is _____ .

Example 4   *Adding a Place-holding Zero*

Divide $4x^2 + 3$ by $x + 1$.

Solution

$$x + 1 \overline{\smash{)}4x^2 + 0x + 3}$$

$$\underline{ + 3}$$

1. Think: $\dfrac{4x^2}{x} =$ ___

2. Subtract ___$(x + 1)$.

3. Bring down $+3$. Think: $\dfrac{\boxed{}}{x} =$ ___

4. Subtract ___$(x + 1)$.

5. Remainder is ___ .

Answer The answer is _____ .

Example 5 — *Rewriting in Standard Form*

Divide $m^2 + 3m - 5$ by $6 + 3m$.

Solution First write the divisor $6 + 3m$ in standard form as $3m + 6$.

1. Think: $\dfrac{m^2}{3m} = $ _____

$3m + 6\overline{)m^2 + 3m - 5}$

$\qquad\qquad\qquad -5$

2. Subtract _____ $(3m + 6)$.

3. Bring down -5. Think: $\dfrac{\square}{3m} = $ _____ .

4. Subtract _____ $(3m + 6)$.

5. Remainder is _____ .

Answer The answer is _____ .

✔ *Checkpoint* **Divide.**

1. Divide $x^2 + 5x - 9$ by $x + 2$.	**2.** Divide $4m^2 + 8$ by $m - 3$.

Rational Equations and Functions

Goals • Solve rational equations.
• Graph rational functions.

VOCABULARY

Rational equation

Rational function

Hyperbola

Center of a hyperbola

Asymptote

Example 1 *Cross Multiplying*

$$\frac{4}{y+4} = \frac{y}{3}$$ **Write original equation.**

$$4(\underline{\quad}) = y(\underline{\qquad})$$ **Cross multiply.**

$$\underline{\quad} = \underline{\qquad}$$ **Simplify.**

$$0 = \underline{\qquad\qquad}$$ **Write in standard form.**

$$0 = (\underline{\qquad})(\underline{\qquad})$$ **Factor right side.**

Answer If you set each factor equal to 0, you see that the solutions are ____ and __. Check both solutions in the original equation.

Example 2   *Multiplying by the LCD*

$$\frac{3}{x} + \frac{1}{4} = \frac{5}{2x}$$ The LCD is ____.

$$\underline{\quad} \cdot \frac{3}{x} + \underline{\quad} \cdot \frac{1}{4} = \underline{\quad} \cdot \frac{5}{2x}$$ Multiply each side by ____

$$\underline{\quad\quad} = \underline{\quad}$$ Simplify.

$$x = \underline{\quad}$$ Simplify.

Check $\dfrac{3}{\boxed{}} + \dfrac{1}{4} \stackrel{?}{=} \dfrac{5}{2(\boxed{})}$ Substitute ____ for *x*.

$$\underline{\quad} = \underline{\quad}$$ Simplify.

Example 3   *Factoring to Find the LCD*

Solve $\dfrac{2}{y+2} + 1 = \dfrac{6}{y^2 + y - 2}$.

Solution The denominator $y^2 + y - 2$ factors as (_____)(_____
so the LCD is (_____)(_____). Multiply each side of the equation
by (_____)(_____).

$$\frac{2(\boxed{})(\boxed{})}{y+2} + 1 \cdot (\underline{\quad})(\underline{\quad}) = \frac{6(\boxed{})(\boxed{})}{(\boxed{})(\boxed{})}$$

$$2(\underline{\quad}) + (\underline{\quad})(\underline{\quad}) = \underline{\quad}$$

$$\underline{\quad\quad\quad} = \underline{\quad}$$

$$\underline{\quad\quad\quad} = \underline{\quad}$$

$$\underline{\quad\quad\quad} = \underline{\quad}$$

$$\underline{\quad\quad\quad} = \underline{\quad}$$

Answer The solutions are ____ and ____. Check both solutions in the
original equation.

✔ Checkpoint Solve the equation.

1. $\dfrac{9}{y-3} = \dfrac{y}{2}$	2. $\dfrac{5}{x} + \dfrac{2}{5} = \dfrac{3}{x}$

RATIONAL FUNCTIONS WHOSE GRAPHS ARE HYPERBOLAS

The graph of the rational function

$$y = \frac{a}{x-h} + k \text{ is a } \underline{\hspace{3cm}}$$

whose center is (___ , ___).

The vertical and horizontal lines through the center are the _____ of the hyperbola.

An asymptote is a line that the graph _____ . While the distance between the graph and the line approaches ____ , the asymptote is _____ .

Branches of the hyperbola

Center (h, k)

Asymptotes

Example 4 *Graphing a Rational Function*

Sketch the graph of $y = \dfrac{1}{x} - 3$.

Solution Think of the function as $y = \dfrac{1}{x-0} + (-3)$. You can see that the center is (___ , ____). The asymptotes can be drawn as dashed lines through the center. Make a table of values then plot the points and connect them with two smooth branches.

x	−4	−2	−1	−0.5
y				

x	0	0.5	1	2	4
y					

> If you have drawn a hyperbola correctly, it should be symmetric about the center (h, k). For instance, in Example 4 the points (1, −2), and (−1, −4) are the same distance from the center, but in opposite directions.

Words to Review

Give an example of the vocabulary word.

Proportion	Extremes of a proportion
Means of a proportion	Extraneous solution
Inverse variation	Rational number
Rational expression	Least common denominator
Rational equation	Rational function
Hyperbola	Center of a hyperbola

Review your notes and Chapter 11 by using the Chapter Review on pages 700–702 of your textbook.

12.1 Functions Involving Square Roots

Goals • Evaluate and graph a function involving square roots.
• Use square root functions to model real-life problems.

VOCABULARY

Square root function

Example 1 *Graphing y = a√x*

Sketch the graph of $y = 3\sqrt{x}$. Give the domain and range.

Solution

The radicand of a square root is always _____, so the domain is the set of all _____ numbers. Make a table of values. Then plot the points and connect them with a smooth curve.

x	y
0	$y = 3\sqrt{0} =$ _____
1	$y = 3\sqrt{1} =$ _____
2	$y = 3\sqrt{2} \approx$ _____
3	$y = 3\sqrt{3} \approx$ _____
4	$y = 3\sqrt{4} =$ _____
5	$y = 3\sqrt{5} \approx$ _____

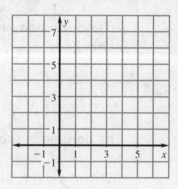

Both the domain and range are all the _____ numbers.

Example 2 *Graphing* $y = \sqrt{x} + k$

Find the domain and range of $y = \sqrt{x} + 2$. Then sketch its graph.

The domain is the set of all _____ numbers. The range is
the set of all numbers that are greater than or equal to ___ . Make
table of values, plot the points, and connect them with a smooth
curve.

x	y	
0	$y = \sqrt{0} + 2 =$	_____
1	$y = \sqrt{1} + 2 =$	_____
2	$y = \sqrt{2} + 2 \approx$	_____
4	$y = \sqrt{4} + 2 =$	_____
6	$y = \sqrt{6} + 2 \approx$	_____

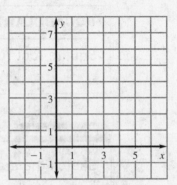

Example 3 *Graphing* $y = \sqrt{x - h}$

Find the domain and range of $y = \sqrt{x - 2}$. Then sketch its graph.

To find the domain, find the values of x for which the radicand is
nonnegative.

$x - 2 \geq 0$ Write an inequality for the domain.

$x \geq$ ___   Add ___ to each side.

The domain is the set of all numbers that are greater than or equal
to ___ . The range is the set of all _____ numbers. Make a
table of values, plot the points, and connect them with a smooth
curve.

x	y	
2	$y = \sqrt{2 - 2} =$	_____
3	$y = \sqrt{3 - 2} =$	_____
4	$y = \sqrt{4 - 2} \approx$	_____
6	$y = \sqrt{6 - 2} =$	_____
8	$y = \sqrt{8 - 2} \approx$	_____

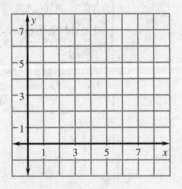

✓ Checkpoint Find the domain and range of the function. Then sketch its graph.

---

1. $y = -3\sqrt{x}$

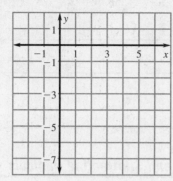

---

2. $y = \sqrt{x} - 2$

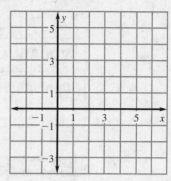

Find the domain and range of the function.

---

3. $y = -\sqrt{x - 4}$

---

4. $y = \sqrt{x - \dfrac{2}{3}}$

Operations with Radical Expression

Goal • Add, subtract, multiply, and divide radical expressions.

VOCABULARY

Conjugates

Example 1 *Adding and Subtracting Radicals*

a. $4\sqrt{3} + 2\sqrt{7} - 9\sqrt{3} = \underline{}\sqrt{3} + 2\sqrt{7}$ Subtract like radical

b. $3\sqrt{5} - \sqrt{20} = 3\sqrt{5} - \sqrt{\underline{} \cdot \underline{}}$ Perfect square facto

$= 3\sqrt{5} - \sqrt{\underline{}} \cdot \sqrt{\underline{}}$ Use product propert

$= 3\sqrt{5} - \underline{}$ Simplify.

$= \underline{}$ Subtract like radical

✔ *Checkpoint* **Simplify the expression.**

1. $5\sqrt{6} + 4\sqrt{6}$	**2.** $4\sqrt{5} - 7\sqrt{5}$
3. $6\sqrt{2} + \sqrt{50}$	**4.** $8\sqrt{7} - \sqrt{28}$

Example 2 **Multiplying Radicals**

a. $\sqrt{3} \cdot \sqrt{27} =$ _____   Use product property.

      $=$ ___   Simplify.

b. $\sqrt{5}(3 - \sqrt{3}) =$ ____ $\cdot 3 -$ ____ $\cdot \sqrt{3}$ Use distributive property.

      $=$ _____   Use product property.

c. $(1 + \sqrt{6})^2 = 1^2 +$ _____ $+ ($____$)^2$ Use square of a binomial pattern.

      $=$ _____   Evaluate powers.

      $=$ _____   Simplify.

d. $(\sqrt{m} - n)(\sqrt{m} + n) =$ _____ $-$ ___   Use sum and difference pattern.

      $=$ _____   Simplify.

A simplified fraction does not have a radical in the denominator. To simplify radical expressions, you may be able to use conjugates or write an equivalent expression with a perfect square under the radical sign in the denominator.

Example 3 **Simplifying Radicals**

a. $\dfrac{2}{\sqrt{7}} = \dfrac{2}{\sqrt{7}} \cdot$ ____   Multiply numerator and denominator by ____.

      $=$ _____   Multiply fractions.

      $=$ _____   Simplify.

b. $\dfrac{1}{\sqrt{a} + b} = \dfrac{1}{\sqrt{a} + b} \cdot$ _____   Multiply numerator and denominator by the conjugate.

      $=$ _____   Multiply fractions.

      $=$ _____   Simplify.

✓ Checkpoint Simplify the expression.

5. $\sqrt{2}(\sqrt{7} - 4)$	**6.** $(2 - \sqrt{7})^2$
7. $\dfrac{4}{\sqrt{11}}$	**8.** $\dfrac{1}{4 + \sqrt{2}}$

Example 4   *Checking Quadratic Formula Solutions*

Check that $3 + \sqrt{6}$ is a solution of $x^2 - 6x + 3 = 0$.

You can check the solution by substituting into the equation.

$$x^2 - 6x + 3 = 0 \qquad \text{Write original equatio}$$

$$(\underline{\hspace{2cm}})^2 - 6(\underline{\hspace{1.5cm}}) + 3 \overset{?}{=} 0 \qquad \text{Substitute for } x.$$

$$\underline{\hspace{5cm}} + 3 \overset{?}{=} 0 \qquad \text{Multiply.}$$

$$\underline{\hspace{1cm}} = 0 \qquad \text{Solution is} \underline{\hspace{2cm}}$$

✓ Checkpoint Solve the quadratic equation. Check the solution.

9. $x^2 + 8x + 2$

Solving Radical Equations

Goals • Solve a radical equation.
• Use radical equations to solve real-life problems.

SQUARING BOTH SIDES OF AN EQUATION

Suppose a and b are algebraic expressions.

If $a = b$, then $a^2 = b^2$.   **Example:** $\sqrt{4} = 2$, so $(\sqrt{4})^2 = 2^2$.

Example 1   *Solving a Radical Equation*

Solve $\sqrt{x} - 5 = 0$.

Solution

$\sqrt{x} - 5 = 0$	Write original equation.
$\sqrt{x} = \underline{}$	Add ___ to each side.
$(\underline{})^2 = \underline{}^2$	Square each side.
$x = \underline{}$	Simplify.

Answer The solution is ____. Check the solution in the original equation.

Example 2   *Solving a Radical Equation*

To solve the equation $\sqrt{3x - 6} + 4 = 7$, you need to isolate the radical expression first.

$\sqrt{3x - 6} + 4 = 7$	Write original equation.
$\sqrt{3x - 6} = \underline{}$	Subtract ___ from each side.
$(\underline{})^2 = \underline{}^2$	Square each side.
$\underline{} - \underline{} = \underline{}$	Simplify.
$\underline{} = \underline{}$	Add ___ to each side.
$x = \underline{}$	Divide each side by ___ .

Answer The solution is ___ . Check the solution in the original equation.

Example 3 *Checking for Extraneous Solutions*

Solve the equation.

a. $\sqrt{x + 6} = x$ b. $\sqrt{x} + 11 = 0$

Solution

a. $\sqrt{x + 6} = x$ Write original equation.

     $(\underline{\hspace{1.5cm}})^2 = \underline{\hspace{0.5cm}}^2$ Square each side.

     $\underline{\hspace{0.5cm}} + \underline{\hspace{0.5cm}} = \underline{\hspace{0.5cm}}^2$ Simplify.

     $0 = \underline{\hspace{3cm}}$ Write in standard form.

     $0 = \underline{\hspace{3cm}}$ Factor.

     $x = \underline{\hspace{0.5cm}}$ or $x = \underline{\hspace{1cm}}$ Zero-product property

Check Substitute $\underline{\hspace{0.5cm}}$ and $\underline{\hspace{1cm}}$ in the original equation.

$\sqrt{\underline{\hspace{0.5cm}} + 6} \stackrel{?}{=} \underline{\hspace{0.5cm}}$ $\sqrt{\underline{\hspace{1cm}} + 6} \stackrel{?}{=} \underline{\hspace{1cm}}$

$\underline{\hspace{2cm}}$ $\underline{\hspace{2cm}}$

Answer The only solution is $\underline{\hspace{0.5cm}}$, because $x = \underline{\hspace{1cm}}$ is not a solution.

b. $\sqrt{x} + 11 = 0$ Write original equation.

     $\sqrt{x} = \underline{\hspace{1cm}}$ Subtract $\underline{\hspace{0.5cm}}$ from each side.

     $(\underline{\hspace{1cm}})^2 = (\underline{\hspace{1cm}})^2$ Square each side.

     $x = \underline{\hspace{1cm}}$ Simplify.

Answer $\sqrt{\underline{\hspace{1cm}}} + 11 \neq 0$, so the equation has no solution.

✔ *Checkpoint* Solve the equation. Check for extraneous solution

1. $\sqrt{x} - 13 = 0$	2. $\sqrt{x} + 15 = 0$

✔ Checkpoint Solve the equation. Check for extraneous solutions.

3. $\sqrt{4x - 8} + 2 = 6$	4. $\sqrt{2x + 3} = x$

Example 4   *Using a Geometric Mean*

The *geometric mean* of a and b is $\sqrt{ab}$. If the geometric mean of a and 4 is 8, what is the value of a?

Solution

$\text{Geometric mean} = \sqrt{ab}$

$\underline{} = \sqrt{\underline{}a}$ Substitute.

$\underline{}^2 = (\underline{})^2$ Square each side.

$\underline{} = \underline{}$ Simplify.

$\underline{} = a$ Solve for a.

✔ Checkpoint Two numbers and their geometric mean are given. Find the value of a.

5. 6 and a; 18	6. 36 and a; 12

12.4 Completing the Square

Goals • Solve a quadratic equation by completing the square.
• Choose a method for solving a quadratic equation.

COMPLETING THE SQUARE

To complete the square of the expression $x^2 + bx$, add the square
of half the coefficient of x.

$$x^2 + bx + \left(\frac{b}{2}\right)^2 = \left(x + \frac{b}{2}\right)^2$$

Example 1   *Completing the Square*

What term should you add to $x^2 + 12x$ so that the result
is a perfect square?

The coefficient of x is ___, so you should add $\left(\dfrac{\boxed{}}{2}\right)^2$, or ___,
the expression.

$$x^2 + 12x + \left(\frac{\boxed{}}{2}\right)^2 = x^2 + 12x + \underline{\quad} = (x + \underline{\quad})^2$$

Example 2   *Solving a Quadratic Equation*

Solve $x^2 + 6x = 16$ by completing the square.

$$x^2 + 6x = 16 \qquad\qquad \text{Write original equation.}$$

$$x^2 + 6x + \underline{\quad}^2 = 16 + \underline{\quad}^2 \qquad \text{Add, } \left(\frac{\boxed{}}{2}\right)^2, \text{ or } \underline{\quad}^2, \text{ to each s}$$

$$(x + \underline{\quad})^2 = \underline{\quad} \qquad\qquad \text{Write left side as perfect square.}$$

$$x + \underline{\quad} = \pm \underline{\quad} \qquad\qquad \text{Find square root of each side.}$$

$$x = -\underline{\quad} \pm \underline{\quad} \qquad\qquad \text{Subtract } \underline{\quad} \text{ from each side.}$$

$$x = \underline{\quad} \text{ or } x = \underline{\quad} \qquad\qquad \text{Simplify.}$$

Answer The solutions are ___ and ___. Check these in the original
equation to see that both are solutions.

Example 3 *The Leading Coefficient is Not 1*

Solve $2x^2 - 6x - 7 = 0$ by completing the square.

Solution

$$2x^2 - 6x - 7 = 0$$ Write original equation.

$$2x^2 - 6x = \_\_\_$$ Add ___ to each side.

$$x^2 - \_\_x = \frac{\_\_}{\_\_}$$ Divide each side by __.

$$x^2 - \_\_x + \left(-\frac{\boxed{}}{2}\right)^2 = \frac{\_\_}{\_\_} + \frac{\_\_}{\_\_}$$ Add $\left(-\dfrac{\boxed{}}{2}\right)^2$, or ___, to each side.

$$\left(x - \frac{\boxed{}}{2}\right)^2 = \frac{\_\_}{\_\_}$$ Write left side as perfect square.

$$\frac{\_\_\_\_}{} = \frac{\_\_\_\_}{}$$ Find square root of each side.

$$x = \frac{\_\_\_\_}{} \frac{\_\_}{}$$ Add __ to each side.

Answer The solutions are $\dfrac{\_\_\_\_}{} \approx \_\_\_\_$ and $\dfrac{\_\_\_\_}{} \approx \_\_\_\_$.

✔ *Checkpoint* **Solve the equation by completing the square.**

1. $x^2 + 8x = 48$	**2.** $2x^2 - 10x - 5 = 0$

METHODS FOR SOLVING $ax^2 + bx + c = 0$

Method	Lesson	Comments
Finding Square Roots	9.1	Efficient way to solve $ax^2 + c = 0$.
Graphing	9.4	Can be used for *any* quadratic equation. May give only approximate solutions.
Using the Quadratic Formula	9.5	Can be used for *any* quadratic equation. Always gives exact solutions of the equation.
Factoring	10.5– 10.8	Efficient way to solve the quadratic equation if the quadratic expression can be factored easily.
Completing the Square	12.4	Can be used for *any* quadratic equation but is simplest to apply when $a = 1$ and b is an even number.

Example 4   *Choosing a Solution Method*

Choose a method to solve the quadratic equation. Explain.

a. $5x^2 - 20 = 0$ **b.** $2x^2 - x - 4 = 0$

Solution

a. Because this quadratic equation has the form $ax^2 + c = 0$, it i most efficiently solved by _____.

b. Because this quadratic equation is not easily factored and the leading coefficient is not 1, it is most efficiently solved by using the _____ or by _____.

✔ *Checkpoint* **Choose a method to solve the quadratic equation. Explain your choice.**

3. $x^2 + 4x = 7$	**4.** $x^2 - 2x - 3 = 0$

12.5 The Pythagorean Theorem and Its Converse

Goal • Use the Pythagorean theorem and its converse.

VOCABULARY

Hypotenuse

Hypothesis, Conclusion

Converse

THE PYTHAGOREAN THEOREM

If a triangle is a right triangle, then the sum of the squares of the lengths of the legs a and b equals the square of the length of the hypotenuse c.

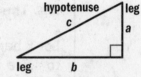

$$a^2 + b^2 = c^2$$

Example 1 *Using the Pythagorean Theorem*

Given $a = 5$ and $b = 12$, find c.

$a^2 + b^2 = c^2$

____ + ____ $= c^2$

_____ $= c^2$

_____ $= c$

_____ $= c$

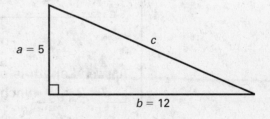

Example 2   *Using the Pythagorean Theorem*

Given $a = 4$ and $c = 9$, find b.

$$a^2 + b^2 = c^2$$

$$\underline{} + b^2 = \underline{}$$

$$b^2 = \underline{}$$

$$b^2 = \underline{}$$

$$b = \underline{} \text{, or about } \underline{}$$

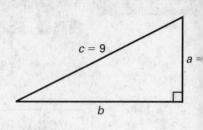

✔ **Checkpoint** Find the missing length of the right triangle if a and b are the lengths of the legs and c is the length of the hypotenuse.

1. $a = 8, b = 15$	**2.** $a = 10, c = 20$

Example 3   *Using the Pythagorean Theorem*

A right triangle has one leg that is 2 inches longer than the oth[er] leg. The hypotenuse is 10 inches. Find the missing lengths.

Let x be the length of the shorter leg. Use the Pythagorean theore[m] to solve for x.

$$a^2 + b^2 = c^2 \qquad \text{Write Pythagorean theorem.}$$

$$\underline{} + \underline{} = \underline{} \qquad \text{Substitute for } a, b, \text{ and } c.$$

$$\underline{} = \underline{} \qquad \text{Simplify.}$$

$$\underline{} = \underline{} \qquad \text{Write in standard form.}$$

$$\underline{} = \underline{} \qquad \text{Factor.}$$

$$x = \underline{} \text{ or } x = \underline{} \qquad \text{Zero-product property}$$

Answer Length is positive. The sides have lengths __ inches and __ + 2 = __ inches.

✅ **Checkpoint** Find each missing length.

3. 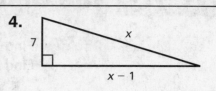 13, $x - 7$, x	**4.** 7, x, $x - 1$

CONVERSE OF THE PYTHAGOREAN THEOREM

If a triangle has side lengths a, b, and c such that $a^2 + b^2 = c^2$, then the triangle is a right triangle.

Example 4 *Determining Right Triangles*

Determine whether the given lengths are sides of a right triangle.

a. 2, 2.1, 2.9   **b.** 6, 8, 11

Solution Use the converse of the Pythagorean theorem.

a. The lengths _____ sides of a right triangle because
$2^2 + 2.1^2 =$ __ + ____ = ____ __ 2.9^2.

b. The lengths _____ sides of a right triangle because
$6^2 + 8^2 =$ __ + __ = ____ __ 11^2.

✅ **Checkpoint** Determine whether the given lengths are sides of a right triangle.

5. 3.9, 8.1, 8.9	**6.** 2.7, 3.6, 4.5

12.6 The Distance and Midpoint Formula

Goals
- Find the distance between two points.
- Find the midpoint between two points.

VOCABULARY

Midpoint

THE DISTANCE FORMULA

The distance d between the points (x_1, y_1) and (x_2, y_2) is

$$d = \sqrt{(x_2 - x_1)^2 + (y_2 - y_1)^2}.$$

Example 1 *Finding the Distance Between Two Points*

Find the distance between (2, 4) and (4, −3).

To find the distance, use the distance formula.

$$d = \sqrt{(x_2 - x_1)^2 + (y_2 - y_1)^2}$$ Write distance formula.

$$= \sqrt{(4 - \underline{})^2 + (\underline{} - 4)^2}$$ Substitute.

$$= \underline{}$$ Simplify.

$$\approx \underline{}$$ Use a calculator.

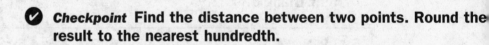 **Checkpoint** Find the distance between two points. Round the result to the nearest hundredth.

1. (3, 1), (−5, 2)	**2.** (−4, 5), (6, −2)

Example 2 *Checking a Right Triangle*

Decide whether the points (1, 0), (3, −1), and
(4, 6) are vertices of a right triangle.

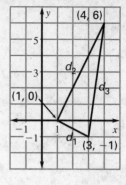

Solution

Use the distance formula to find the lengths
of the three sides.

$$d_1 = \sqrt{(3 - \underline{})^2 + (\underline{} - 0)^2} = \underline{}$$

$$= \underline{}$$

$$d_2 = \sqrt{(\underline{} - 1)^2 + (6 - \underline{})^2} = \underline{} = \underline{}$$

$$d_3 = \underline{} = \underline{} = \underline{}$$

Next find the sum of the squares of the lengths of the two
shorter sides.

$$d_1{}^2 + d_2{}^2 = \underline{} + \underline{} \qquad \text{Substitute for } d_1 \text{ and } d_2.$$

$$= \underline{} + \underline{} \qquad\qquad \text{Simplify.}$$

$$= \underline{} \qquad\qquad\qquad \text{Add.}$$

The sum of the squares of the lengths of the shorter sides is ____,
which _____ the square of the length of the longest side,
(_____)^2.

Answer The given points _____ vertices of a right triangle.

✔ *Checkpoint* **Decide whether the points are vertices of a right
triangle.**

3. (1, 0), (7, 0), (7, 5)	**4.** (0, 4), (2, −2), (5, −1)

THE MIDPOINT FORMULA

The midpoint between (x_1, y_1) and (x_2, y_2) is $\left(\dfrac{x_1 + x_2}{2}, \dfrac{y_1 + y_2}{2}\right)$.

Example 3   *Finding the Midpoint Between Two Points*

Find the midpoint between $(-3, -1)$ and $(2, 4)$. Use a graph to check the result.

Solution

$$\left(\dfrac{\boxed{} + 2}{2}, \dfrac{\boxed{} + 4}{2}\right) = \left(-\dfrac{\boxed{}}{2}, \dfrac{\boxed{}}{2}\right)$$

Answer The midpoint is _____ .

Check From the graph, you can see that

the point _____ appears halfway

between $(-3, -1)$ and $(2, 4)$. You can also use the distance formula to check that the distances from the midpoint to each given point are equal.

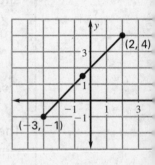

✔ *Checkpoint* **Find the midpoint between the two points.**

5. $(3, 5), (-2, -3)$	**6.** $(-7, 4), (5, -10)$
7. $(-9, -2), (6, -2)$	**8.** $(-6, 9), (2, -5)$

12.7 Trigonometric Ratios

Goals • Use the sine, cosine, and tangent of an angle.
• Use trigonometric ratios in real-life problems.

TRIGONOMETRIC RATIOS

$$\sin A = \frac{\text{side opposite } \angle A}{\text{hypotenuse}} = \frac{a}{c}$$

$$\cos A = \frac{\text{side adjacent to } \angle A}{\text{hypotenuse}} = \frac{b}{c}$$

$$\tan A = \frac{\text{side opposite } \angle A}{\text{side adjacent to } \angle A} = \frac{a}{b}$$

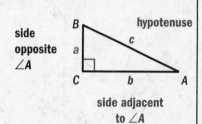

Example 1 *Finding Trigonometric Ratios*

For $\triangle DEF$, find the sine, the cosine, and the tangent of the angle.

a. $\angle D$ **b.** $\angle E$

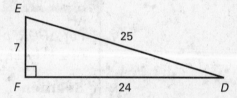

Solution

a. For $\angle D$, the opposite side is ___, and the adjacent side is ___.
The hypotenuse is ___.

$$\sin D = \frac{\text{opposite}}{\text{hypotenuse}} = \underline{\quad} \qquad \cos D = \frac{\text{adjacent}}{\text{hypotenuse}} = \underline{\quad}$$

$$\tan D = \frac{\text{opposite}}{\text{adjacent}} = \underline{\quad}$$

b. For $\angle E$, the opposite side is ___, and the adjacent side is ___.
The hypotenuse is ___.

$$\sin E = \frac{\text{opposite}}{\text{hypotenuse}} = \underline{\quad} \qquad \cos E = \frac{\text{adjacent}}{\text{hypotenuse}} = \underline{\quad}$$

$$\tan E = \frac{\text{opposite}}{\text{adjacent}} = \underline{\quad}$$

Checkpoint Find the sine, the cosine, and the tangent of ∠*D* and of ∠*E*.

1.

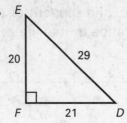

2.

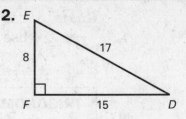

Example 2 **Solving a Right Triangle**

For Δ*PQR*, *p* = 9 and the measure of ∠*P* is 13°. Find the length *q*.

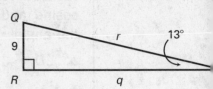

Solution

You are given the side opposite ∠*P*, and you need to find the leng of the _____.

tan *P* = _____   **Definition of tangent**

tan ____ = _____   **Substitute for *p* and ∠*P*.**

q = _____   **Solve for *q*.**

q ≈ _____   **Use a calculator or a table.**

q ≈ _____   **Simplify.**

Answer The length of *q* is about _____ units.

Example 3   *Solving a Right Triangle*

For $\triangle PQR$, $p = 9$ and the measure of $\angle P$ is $13°$. Find the length r.

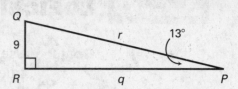

Solution

You are given the side opposite $\angle P$, and you need to find the length of the _____.

$\sin P = \underline{\hspace{3cm}}$	**Definition of sine**
$\sin \underline{\hspace{1cm}} = \dfrac{\underline{\hspace{1cm}}}{\underline{\hspace{1cm}}}$	**Substitute for p and $\angle P$.**
$r = \underline{\hspace{2cm}}$	**Solve for r.**
$r \approx \underline{\hspace{2cm}}$	**Use a calculator or a table.**
$r \approx \underline{\hspace{1cm}}$	**Simplify.**

Answer The length of r is about ____ units.

Check You can use the Pythagorean theorem to check that the results in Examples 1 and 2 are reasonable. Because the values of q and r were rounded, the check will not be exact.

$p^2 + q^2 = r^2$	**Pythagorean theorem**
$9^2 + \underline{\hspace{1.5cm}}^2 \overset{?}{=} \underline{\hspace{1cm}}^2$	**Substitute for p, q, and r.**
$\underline{\hspace{3cm}} \approx \underline{\hspace{1.5cm}}$	**Side lengths are approximately** $\underline{\hspace{2cm}}$.

✔ *Checkpoint* **Complete the following exercise.**

3. For $\triangle ABC$, $a = 19$ and the measure of $\angle A$ is $41°$. Find the length of c.

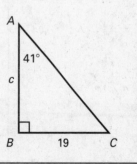

Logical Reasoning: Proof

Goals • Use logical reasoning and proof to prove a statement is true.
• Prove that a statement is false.

VOCABULARY

Postulates or axioms

Theorems

Conjecture

Indirect proof

THE BASIC AXIOMS OF ALGEBRA

Let a, b, and c be real numbers.

Axioms of Addition and Multiplication

Closure: $a + b$ is a _____ number

ab is a _____ number.

Commutative: $a + b = \underline{} + \underline{}$

$ab = \underline{}$

Associative: $(a + b) + c = \underline{} + (\underline{} + \underline{})$

$(ab)c = \underline{}$

Identity: $a + 0 = \underline{}$, $0 + a = \underline{}$

$a(1) = \underline{}$, $1(a) = \underline{}$

Inverse: $a + (-a) = \underline{}$

$a\left(\dfrac{1}{a}\right) = \underline{}$, $a \neq \underline{}$

Axiom Relating Addition and Multiplication

Distributive: $a(b + c) = \underline{} + \underline{}$

$(a + b)c = \underline{} + \underline{}$

Axioms of Equality

Addition: If $a = b$, then $a + \underline{} = b + \underline{}$.

Multiplication: If $a = b$, then $a\underline{} = b\underline{}$.

Substitution: If $a = b$, then a can be substituted for $\underline{}$.

Example 1 *Proving a Theorem*

> When you are proving a new theorem, every step must be justified by an axiom, a definition, given information, or a previously proved theorem.

Use the associative and commutative properties to prove the following theorem.

If a, b, and c are real numbers, then $(a + b) - c = (b - c) + a$.

Solution

$(a + b) - c = \underline{} + (\underline{} - \underline{})$ _____ property

$= (\underline{} - \underline{}) + \underline{}$ _____ property

Example 2 *Conjecture*

Write four examples to show that when $x < 0$ and n is an odd integer, then x^n is negative. Do your examples prove the conjecture that x^n is negative when $x < 0$ and n is an odd integer?

Solution

First, write four examples to show that when $x < 0$ and n is an odd integer, then x^n is negative.

$(-3)^3 =$ _____ $(-2)^5 =$ _____ $(-7)^1 =$ _____ $(-5)^3 =$ ___

This list of examples _____ the conjecture. ____ number of examples can prove the rule is true for every x-value less than zero and for every odd integer n.

Example 3 *Finding a Counterexample*

Assign values to a and b to show that the following conjecture is false.

$$a^2 + b^2 = (a + b)^2$$

Solution

You can choose any values of a and b. For instance, let $a = 2$ and $b = 3$. Evaluate the left side of the equation.

$a^2 + b^2 =$ __^{2} + __^{2} **Substitute for a and b.**

= ____   **Simplify.**

Evaluate the right side of the equation.

$(a + b)^2 = ($__ + __$)^2$ **Substitute for a and b.**

= ____   **Simplify.**

Because ____ $\neq$ ____, you have shown one case in which the conjecture is _____. The counterexample of $a = 2$ and $b = 3$ is sufficient to prove that $a^2 + b^2 = (a + b)^2$ is _____.

Example 4 **Using an Indirect Proof**

Use an indirect proof to prove that $\sqrt{3}$ is an irrational number.

Solution

Assume that $\sqrt{3}$ is _____ irrational. Then $\sqrt{3}$ is _____ and can be written as the quotient of two integers a and b that have no common factors other than 1.

$$\sqrt{3} = \frac{a}{b}$$ Assume $\sqrt{3}$ is a rational number.

$$3 = \frac{a^2}{b^2}$$ Square each side.

$$3\underline{} = a^2$$ Multiply each side by ___.

This implies that 3 is a factor of ____. Therefore 3 is also a factor of ___. (You will prove this in Exercise 25 on page 763 of your Algebra 1 text.) So a can be written as 3c.

$$3b^2 = (3c)^2$$ Substitute 3c for a.

$$3b^2 = \underline{}c^2$$ Simplify.

$$b^2 = \underline{}c^2$$ Divide each side by 3.

This implies that ___ is a factor of b^2 and also a factor of b. So ___ is a factor of both a and b. But this is _____ because a and b have ____ common factors. Therefore it must be _____ that $\sqrt{3}$ is a rational number. So you can conclude that $\sqrt{3}$ _____ an irrational number.

✔ *Checkpoint* **Complete the following exercise.**

1. Assign values to a and b to show that the following conjecture is false.

   $$-(a + b) = -a + b$$

Words to Review

Give an example of the vocabulary word.

Square root function	Conjugates
Complete the square	Pythagorean theorem
Hypotenuse	Legs of a right triangle
Conclusion	Converse
Distance formula	Midpoint between two points
Midpoint formula	Trigonometric ratio
Postulate (or axiom)	Theorem

Review your notes and Chapter 12 by using the Chapter Review on pages 766–768 of your textbook.